PADDY DOYLE

IRON MAN

PADDY DOYLE
IRON MAN

THE TRUE STORY OF BRITAIN'S STRONGEST, FASTEST, HARDEST MAN

JOHN BLAKE

Published by John Blake Publishing Ltd, 3 Bramber Court,
2 Bramber Road, London W14 9PB, England

First published in the UK in hardback in 2002

ISBN 1 904034 23 3

British Library Cataloguing-in-Publication Data: A catalogue record for this book is
available from the British Library.

Design by ENVY

Printed in Great Britain by Creative Print and Design (Wales),
Ebbw Vale, Gwent

1 3 5 7 9 10 8 6 4 2

Papers used by John Blake Publishing Ltd are natural, recyclable products made from
wood grown in sustainable forests. The manufacturing processes conform to the
environmental regulations of the country of origin.

Every attempt has been made to contact the relevant copyright-holders, but some were
untraceable. We would be grateful if the relevant people could contact us.

DEDICATION

This book is dedicated to my mother, Bridget Doyle,
my late father, Patsy Doyle, my late brother, Eddie Doyle, my
brother and sister, Declan and Bridget Doyle, my fiancée, Samantha
Cartwright, my friend and coach, Desi Clifton, my friends Danny
Ryan OBE and Paul Jones, my uncle, John Derwin, my 'coach',
Ralph Farqharson, Wayne Bernstein, all the Birmingham citizens
who have supported me throughout my sporting career, the
Midlands press and media and *The Guinness Book of World
Records/Guinness World Records*.

www.stamina4life.co.uk

CONTENTS

CHAPTER 1

ATTACK!

A REGULAR EVENING. I'm driving down an ordinary street in the suburbs of Birmingham, coming back from a training session at my gym. I've been teaching the martial arts to a group of students and I'm cruising along, my mind on a self-protection course I'm giving the following week at the local adult education centre. Little do I know, I'm about to put my years of training and experience into practice.

Ahead, I can just make out a white car. There are four black guys standing there. Big guys. Tall and big. They flash me down. I decide they must know me from somewhere. Probably one of the local boxing or martial-arts clubs I train at. I pull over. Just as I stop, one of the guys comes running over to me. I can see he's well over six foot. And I can see I don't know him from Adam. By this time the guy is at my window, and so are the others. One of them opens my car door and grabs my arm. 'Get out of the car, quick!' he barks at me.

Well, I'm my own man, always have been, and I tell him where to go. But he's got hold of me and he's pulling my arm. Now, all my natural instincts rise up, and I start punching and kicking out. At the same time I'm out of the car as fast as I can be, so I can have a proper go at this guy. Two more men come at me, then another. Something flashes, glints. But I'm busy; my mind is elsewhere, the adrenalin is flowing. At first I don't feel anything. You don't when you've got eight arms coming at you.

I'm still battling with them when I see one of the guys is wielding a knife. Another has a Stanley knife and he's shoved it into the calf of my leg. The first guy jumps into my car. I can hear him shouting, 'I can't start it! I can't start it!' It must be the cut-out switch. No time to lose. I run over and kick the car door, trapping the man's head between the roof and the side door. I'm angry I've dented my door but it's better than seeing the car disappear down the road.

I turn and run back to the other guys, shouting, 'Come on then!' But I can see they're starting to flap. They're not ready for this kind of confrontation: a driver ready to go for it. Someone says, 'Let's get the hell out of it, quick!' I'm still putting up a fight as the four blokes run away. Four guys don't bother me. I'm doing what I have to do. I'm not going anywhere.

Funny thing was, there were witnesses to all of this. Grown men, standing there, looking out of the windows of their houses. When the fight had finished, these people went back to their armchairs and sat back down to watch their TVs. Not that I needed any help with the situation. But it would have been OK by me if someone had phoned the police. No one did. Turns out later, in one of the police statements, that these respectable householders thought I was messing about with those guys, having a laugh.

I reckon it was a cop-out. People don't want to get involved, don't want to know. They want to protect themselves. Don't tell me you can't see from your window who's messing about and who isn't. I didn't need their help. All I'd wanted them to do was ring the police so they could catch the guys, instead of me just chasing after them. Then I could have stood up in court and pointed out who'd stabbed me.

The police officer looked at me and shook his head, as if to say, 'What can you do? People just don't want to help out these days.' Not long after that I managed to acquire one or two addresses, and I made it all good for them. It was about four or five o'clock in the morning when I knocked on their doors. I might have scared them a little, got them out of bed, something like that. Well, it's a mental game.

And they might have walked out the next day and found various objects around their front doors. Maybe they had to move house. I might have scared them out of their own homes. They might have thought I'd have done their heads in. Maybe they'll help someone out next time.

But, the night of the attack, I went to bed and slept like a log. All those years of military training in the Paras, the security work, the skills I'd acquired in boxing and the martial arts, the fitness and endurance records I'd set and the courses in self-protection I'd given to others: they'd all paid off that night. I'd done what I had to do. I saw those attackers off. They ran like cowards, and they didn't get my car. And I wouldn't hesitate to do it again.

Next time I'll probably hospitalise the aggressors. They may never breathe again. At the time there was an element of surprise when they attacked me, but it's been rehearsed now. If anybody tries to take my car off me again, they'll be six foot under. A local reporter rang me up not long after the incident. He'd seen the articles in the *Sun* and the *Daily Star* about how I'd defended myself. He asked me, 'What would you do if you saw those guys again?' I gave him a quick résumé, mentioning axes and saws, limbs and acid, plus certain burying techniques. He didn't print my reply.

All the confidence and fitness that goes with being a champion had seen me through that night. Over the previous fourteen years I'd broken some of the world's toughest fighting and endurance records. I'd featured in *The Guinness Book of World Records* every year for twelve years, run London Marathons with forty-four-pound backpacks, broken stamina records on television and overseas; I'd done it all. But there was one world record left that I wanted to beat. Just one more before I felt I could retire. It would be my one hundred and fourteenth record challenge. A ten-eventer with all the press and television there. The decision to retire had been a tough one but, at the age of thirty-seven, I wanted to finish my record-breaking career without serious injury, in competition or training. On 25 November 2001, at the Fox Hollies Leisure Centre in Birmingham, I had to go out at the top.

I was born Patrick Daniel Doyle on 1 March 1964 at the Queen Elizabeth Hospital in Birmingham. My parents, Patrick and Bridget Doyle, were living in Erdington at the time, an area north of Birmingham city centre, near Spaghetti Junction.

My parents had come across to England, with other members of their family, from Ireland. My mother was a Derwin and came from Rathmines in the Dublin mountains. My father came from a farming background in County Wexford. My father's mother had died not long after he was born, and a couple of years after that his father died. So he never really got to know his parents. Just one of those things, a sad circumstance.

He was raised on a farm with his cousins by his uncles and aunts. When he was a young man he moved to Dublin to find work, and that's where he met my mother. I'm not sure how they met. Probably at a dance. They loved dancing.

My mother had the family background my dad had lacked: a real father and mother, three brothers and three sisters. People had big families back then. But, quite often, some of the children died young. My mother's background was more of a city upbringing. Rathmines is now a posh part of Dublin. Very nice, a very conservative area. Her mother was a seamstress, I think, and my grandfather was into a bit of everything: taxi-driving, building work, stuff like that.

My maternal grandfather was a big man, and something of an

athlete as well. He joined the Irish Defence Force, the Irish army, for a dare in 1914 and was billeted in Wales. The first night he was there he was looking for somewhere to sleep and he stuck his head in a tent and got a boot on his head for his trouble. Most people would have left it at that, but he followed the soldiers in that tent, as best he could, and they were all sent to Italy to fight. One night he was sitting round with some other soldiers, swapping tales, when a bloke said, 'I'll never forget the night a fellow put his face in our tent and I gave him the boot, right on the head.'

My grandfather sprang up. 'Oh-ho!' he said. 'I'm your man!' The other guy jumped up and went outside the tent with him. They had a pretty good fight, and there was an officer looking on as they fought. Like my grandfather, the other fellow was a good scrapper, but the fight went my grandfather's way.

Not long after that the army boxing tournaments came up and my grandfather saw his name was on the list of bouts. He deleted it. He'd never boxed in a ring in his life. But the officer who'd seen him fight that night came up to him and said, 'Did you cross your name out?'

My grandfather said, 'I did.'

The officer said, 'I put your name on the list. You can do it, you know. You can win. And I'll be your second.' And that's how my grandfather got into the ring. I suppose his fighting methods would have been different from other people's. They wouldn't have been by the book, but they wouldn't have been foul either. He became the army's Amateur Heavyweight Champion. He only ever went two rounds, even though a fight goes to three. He'd won by then.

He loved horses, as well, and fought in cavalry charges in Russia. He said the Russians were lovely people. But he was out there to do a job. My Uncle John used to ask him if he'd ever killed anyone. My grandfather would never say.

Grandfather was a bit of a character, by all accounts, and I think I've inherited his personality. He was a gentleman but nobody stood on his toes. He was over six foot one, which was tall at the time, and stocky and strong. My first cousins take after him: very tall, six-footers. My side of the family drew the short straw; we're the shorter ones. Grandfather Derwin won a number of cups and medals and my uncles in Ireland have kept them. As well as being a good amateur boxer, he was a sprinter and a competitive cross-country runner at a high level. But there was no money in sport in those days. Even today, I don't believe there's much money in cross-country running.

But sport isn't about money. It's the winning that counts. It's the will to win, regardless of the level you're at. Until my retirement in November 2001, I competed in a number of minority sports, from circuit training to strength, speed and stamina, from boxing to the martial arts. I didn't focus on just one particular strength or aspect of my body. I was an all-rounder. I excelled in several disciplines. My grandfather would challenge people to run against him and I was just the same; I'd check out the record books, looking for a challenge. If I thought I could beat a record, I'd train for it and go for it. I got my competitive spirit from my grandfather; he had that sporting will. He was a hard character, a tough one. I think that's how you had to be in those days to get on. And I've inherited that from him too: the capacity to focus, to be disciplined. He had a mindset and the level of commitment that I've got, so I reckon it's in the genes.

Grandfather Derwin ran his own taxi business in Dublin. He made golf clubs, patented a car battery carrier and he supported seven children. He was a goer and trier. When I'd broken a record for, say, fitness and endurance, my uncles and aunts would say, 'You've got that fighting spirit from your grandad.' They could see his approach to a sporting challenge in my attitude. They saw it in my body language, the way I projected myself and my physical mannerisms. A while back I saw a photograph of the man himself: broken nose and cauliflower ears, probably from the boxing. Cauliflower ears are the result of blood clots that form when your ears are pounded. You don't see many these days because people wear head guards. My nose was broken in a fight, but it was a clean break and it was reset.

I saw some of Grandad's trophies about five or six years ago. His medals are in Dublin with one of his sons. I only ever saw my grandfather once, that I remember. He had a full face like me, a thick neck, as I have, and he was muscular, as I am. He looked at me, all those feet below him, and I looked up at him. I was probably about three or four, and you don't hold conversations with people when you're that age. He must have been in his seventies or even his eighties then, because my mother had me late in life. So I never really knew him.

Mum was forty-four when I arrived. I wasn't planned. My brother and sister are around ten years older than me. I can see myself in my mother, as well as in my grandad, both physically and mentally. Like my grandad and me, my mother is a stubborn character. And she was a competitor too. She was a ballroom dancing champion in Ireland in her younger days. She won a cup. I think it was David Nixon who presented her with the trophy. My dad used to dance too. And that's probably where they met, on the dance floor.

My father died in 1985, when I was in the army. My mother's eighty now. She still talks occasionally about her dancing days. When my brother got married recently, she was watching the dancing and reminiscing about her days as a ballroom champion. But she's in a wheelchair now and, I think, because she can't get up and dance and socialise now, it's a bit of a setback for her. She's got the family energy and competitive spirit, and it came out in a feminine way with her dancing. Ballroom dancing competitions are very demanding physically, and you have to commit yourself to train for events. And she did just that. To this day she's mentally active and strong-minded. Nothing's changed with her; she doesn't miss a trick. She's still Mum. Nobody can put one over her, but it could be the other way round. She's the old school and she's good at getting attention. She likes it, just as she did when she was dancing. She likes people around her. She's a social person.

My dad was a sociable person too. He loved people and got on with everybody. Never had any enemies. My oldest brother, Declan, was born in Ireland and not long after that, in the early fifties, the family came to England to look for work. They went to Aston, which is now the rough part of Birmingham. My mum used to tell me that when they first came over, there were notices in the boarding houses saying, 'No dogs or Irish allowed'. It was like that then. But the country needed extra labour after the Second World War and my father got work with some engineering companies, and eventually we moved to Erdington.

Then my sister Bridget was born and my brother Eddie came along after that. I was the afterthought in 1964. But Eddie was to die young. He drew the short straw and died of cancer when he was thirty-five, leaving five kids. I think his illness might have been related to smoking. There was a gap of about ten years between Eddie and me, so I was almost like an only child. And I got very wild.

A factor in all of this wildness might have been my mum and dad splitting up when I was four years old. That's when things started happening in my life. I went to live with my father. My mum had met someone else and it was decided I should go with my father, probably because I was such a handful. My brothers and sister were that much older, so I was the only one who went to live with Dad. The others were growing up and leaving home around that time, making their own lives. Declan joined the army at sixteen.

Mum moved to another part of Erdington, about three or four miles away. I used to see her every Sunday for four hours, and had a great time. I got a good Sunday lunch as well. Dad found a job with some builders, working on the construction of Spaghetti Junction, the motorway link. He did that for a couple of years and it was during this time that I really started getting wild. But I think

I had a rebellious temperament, even before then. I was always a livewire, from the moment I was born. Always was a problem.

One incident I don't remember, but I'm told happened, was when I was about two or three years old. I picked up my mother's purse. My father had just given her all his wages and she'd put the money in it. I threw the purse on the fire. For days after that we were broke and everyone had to scrape around for food. A year or two after that, I'm told, I couldn't go out to play for some reason. So I climbed the garden wall to get out, fell and broke my arm. I was whipped off to the hospital to get it reset, but that didn't stop me getting into scrapes. I was bolder than other kids of my age and always getting into trouble.

Already I was hanging around bigger boys, about seven or eight years older than me. If they got into some mischief, I'd be there with them. Often the episodes got out of hand and we'd end up damaging property. Things could get violent, even at that age. I ended up behaving like a crazy little kid. Dad used to put me to bed before he went off to work, but I used to get up and slip out of the front door. Some nights my dad would go out on his night shift and as soon as he'd gone I'd sneak out of the house. I'd be out playing, at the age of five, at ten o'clock at night and he didn't know anything about it.

But one night my dad caught me. He was on his way to work and he caught me playing on a motorway with some other lads. The motorway was still being built then and it was a great place to play football.

Sometimes we kids would climb eighty-foot ladders, those big old wooden ones, to get on to the motorway, just for a laugh. I wouldn't do it now. And, during the day, we'd run up and down the motorway link and have the workmen running after us, trying to chase us off. And we'd slide down the ladders again to get away fast. Well, you've got no fear at that age. It was to be the same as I grew older.

CHAPTER 2

BRUISER

ERDINGTON WAS GROWING into a multicultural area at that time, and I used to hang around with a lot of black guys. We lived in Minstead Road and there were a lot of black families in our street. They were good friends of mine, the black kids I grew up with. One day a Jamaican guy, who was married to a white woman, called the police. He'd had a porch built on to his house. I was only about four at the time, but I'd taken all the putty out around his new porch windows. I remember my dad told me off good and proper for that one.

The houses in the area were mostly pre-war semis. My road was a pretty rough one: there were some real characters living there. The police were always going up and down the street because there were so many confrontations between neighbours, black and white. There were a lot of Irish families there, but no Asians. They moved in later, in the late seventies, when there was no longer anywhere for them in Uganda and places like that. It was a working-class road, rough and ready. It's still the same today, I'm told. Someone got shot there a while back.

Our neighbours had some problems with me, as well. They kept hens, and one day I got into the run and smashed all the eggs in there, out of sheer devilment. I don't really know why I did these things. I just thought, Cor, there's some eggs here. I'll smash 'em! About half an hour later I could hear our neighbour going barmy, shouting, 'Who's done this? Who's smashed all me eggs!'

He must have known who it was. I was a known troublemaker in the street. I used to throw bricks and stones through windows and run back into my house, double quick. Or I'd ask for a go on a kid's bike and scoot off with it. I'd go home on it and leave it outside my house. I didn't pinch it, as such. I'd just go inside and forget about it. I wasn't trying to thieve the bike; I was a kid and didn't have the mindset to sell the machine. I just said, 'Can I have a go of your bike?' and then left it in my front garden. Next thing I knew, the kid's parents were speaking to my dad, and I'd get, 'Patrick, what've you been doing?' My dad always called me Patrick. Other lads I knew were getting into trouble too, but I had another outlet for my energy, and that was sport.

I was always interested in competing. I started primary school when I was four, and running and gymnastics interested me right from the beginning. I thoroughly enjoyed gymnastics. It gave me the basic skill that I use today. A lot of the records I've got, such as press-ups, are gymnastics based. I represented the school in junior gymnastic competitions. But I came sixteenth out of thirty regional competitors, and you had to be in the top fifteen to be selected to go forward for the national competition. I wasn't a great gymnast but I was good enough to compete for the school.

I represented the school on other occasions too. I used to run for my junior school at the Midlands Inter School sports days. I came third in a one hundred metres race and second in another when I was about seven years old. I think I received certificates for those but they're lost and gone. The judo certificates I've still got.

Judo was my first activity-based sport. I was eight years old when I was taken along by my cousins to my first lesson. My mother's brother, Uncle John, lived with his family in the same road as us. My uncle and aunt had come over to England with my parents and, although they would eventually go back to Dublin, they brought up their family in Birmingham. I think my uncle could see I had a lot of energy to get rid of. It's possible the adults around me decided I needed to let off steam in a controlled environment.

I've got a lot of respect for my Uncle John. Years later, when my father died, I grew very close to him. He became a father figure to me. I love the guy and there's a real bond between us. He's a hard man and a character, like my grandfather, and I'm told we use similar expressions and our personalities are the same. We put our points across in the same way. He's smaller than me, only five foot three, but he likes sport and follows it avidly. Uncle John's sons were already having judo lessons and I think it was his idea to include me when they went along to the Atled Judo Club in Chester Road, Erdington.

Immediately I loved the idea of contact sports. I found I had a skill or a talent for judo. It was the right sport for me to begin with because it incorporates aggression, and I was always ready to hit something. I loved the idea of my fists coming in contact with someone. But I had no idea I would soon be winning medals and certificates and taking part in regional competitions.

My instructor at the club was a guy called Bob Atkins. I'll never forget him: lovely bloke, brilliant instructor, although I don't know what he's doing now. He had a good way of teaching the sport. He brought on juniors like me, got them to progress and do well. He encouraged us a lot, and the result was I stuck at judo for three or four years.

The classes were held on Friday evenings. I turned up for my first lesson in my ordinary clothes and watched my cousins doing mat work. It was a whole new environment for me and it was exciting at that age to walk into something different. I liked the rolling about and the wrestling, the grappling and holding, and my interest developed from there.

I went back to the class the following week with my new judo outfit and started working for my first grading. Gradings are thorough physical tests which take you up to the next colour belt. I think the gradings in those days were a lot tougher than they are today; the regulations were tighter then. I reckon tests are simpler now, less demanding, softer. Standards change. Going for a grading in the seventies was a lot harder than it is now.

Outside examiners from the old Amateur Judo Association would come along and test us. We started with a white belt and worked, first of all, to get a yellow one. There was about three or four months between each grading. I never failed a grading test, thank God. Even at that age, failure was something to avoid. I didn't like failing. Not in sport.

Funnily enough, I could accept failure on the academic side of my life. It didn't bother me if I failed an English or a maths test at school, but it would have bothered me if I'd had a setback sportswise. I didn't know where sport was going to lead me but, as long as I was doing well in that, I didn't feel bad about classwork. I was a slow learner in school anyway. Some people are born with the ability to learn from books faster than others and some are born with more sporting skills. It's horses for courses. I was quicker on the sports field than the person I sat next to in class. So, in class, I would literally take a back seat.

Judo lessons were my big interest for several years. By the time I was eleven I'd got my green belt and I'd been in about fifteen club competitions, one about every two months. With my gradings, and allowing for injury, which happened even at that age, this was packing quite a bit into two and a half years. One time I was doing mat work and someone swept me back. Something snapped when I landed. I'd broken my ankle.

But the urge to compete was there and I got several certificates in the Midlands Junior Judo Championships. The first one was for the Under-11s Championship on 27 June 1974, where I came fourth in the finals. The following year, in the finals on 3 May, I took the bronze medal. Then, in 1976, I won the silver.

The 1974 championship was my first real taste of competition. I was an orange belt by then, and travelled with the club to a comprehensive school in Walsall. The place was packed; there were a lot of competitors. I'll always remember one of my opponents had me in a neck hold and I wouldn't submit. Eventually the blood supply to my brain was blocked and next thing I was unconscious. I came round on the mat about thirty seconds later. I opened my eyes and wondered where I was for a minute. The medics checked me over. 'Next time,' said the referee, 'Submit.'

OK, I was in the wrong: I should have submitted. But I never give up. I'd rather die than lose. I've always said that. Even at that age, I wouldn't give in. I'd have to be near enough killed first. 'Why didn't you submit?' they asked me.

'Because I didn't want to give in.'

They stood back and looked at me. 'That was a stupid thing to do,' said the coach.

But I was in the last four. I could have got a bronze medal. It was stubbornness. I wanted that medal.

Your body adapts to being pushed around and bruised all over. Maybe your ribs get pummelled, the shins and ankles, the back and the stomach, but it's worth it. I highly recommend judo for toughening up the body. It's an excellent sport. I used it as a stepping stone, four or five years later, to go just that bit further. I wanted a full-contact sport: boxing, punching, to go that extra mile. And that was to capture my interest as much as judo had earlier on. Every time the Olympics came on TV, I'd watch the boxing, the judo and the wrestling. Contact sports are at their highest standard in the Olympics.

* * *

I took a break from judo for about six months when I joined another local club, St John's Gymnastic Club in Erdington. I did this off my own bat and went along every Wednesday evening. The first time I went, they assessed my level of ability. After that they worked on my weak points and turned them into strengths. Gymnastics involves a lot of floor work and balance. Balance was a weak point for me and they helped me improve that. It was something different, which I enjoyed doing, and I ended up being able to do groundwork, including forward and backward rolls, forward somersaults and splits, and balancing on one arm and doing one-arm press-ups.

The club encouraged me to get my BAGA I, II and III from the British Amateur Gymnastics Association. We already did gymnastics at school and I told them I was doing extra gymnastics at a club. This improved my ranking in school gymnastics and, by the time I'd finished primary school, I'd got my BAGA IV and taken part in several school gymnastic exhibitions. I made the finals of the Midlands Schools Championships but I never got into the top fifteen. But, without that outside club coaching, I wouldn't even have made sixteenth place; I probably would have come last. So the club gave me a real lift in gym work.

A lot of people do a sport for a couple of weeks then stop

making the effort. But I always kept at it, trying to reach competition level. I've wanted to come away with the T-shirt, or the experience of the event. So, if I came sixteenth, it was an experience to get to sixteenth. I've never given up. At school I always tried my hardest in PT and gave one hundred per cent, and I got on much better with the PT instructor than I did with the other teachers. His name was Mr Arkinsall. But there was one moment when I didn't please him so much.

I was complaining I hadn't been selected for the school cricket team. I'd always turned up for training and practice but I was never selected to play. Coming back from practice one day, I gave the PT teacher a load of cheek because I hadn't been chosen to play, and he hit me right across the head. I'll never forget it because he was the head teacher as well. It actually did me some good. In those days teachers were allowed to wallop children to discipline them, and I got hit several times by different teachers. Nowadays, if that happens, the parents are down to the school straight away. I disapprove of that. I come from the old school: I had the cane and the slipper on my backside when I got to senior level.

Dad never hit me. He was very soft with me at home. Maybe that gave me more confidence to be bold outside the home. Not that I thought of myself as being out of control or wild. That's the way I was, and it was part of life. It seemed totally natural to me that I was always in trouble. I didn't follow anyone along that path, I was never coerced. But, without knowing it, trouble found me. As soon as I stepped outside the front door a feeling of devilment came over me. We've all done things that have got us into trouble, but I probably took that to the extreme. I attracted certain kinds of friends, normally older than me. They came from a different school in the same area, so no one around me knew what I was getting up to. It was only when the police came to the door that my father knew about it.

I must have been about eight or nine years of age when the law first called on Dad. I'd broken into a youth club with a friend. We smashed a window and got inside and used the phone. That was it really. We were just looking around the place when the caretaker turned up. As he didn't know who was in the building, he phoned the police. Later he said that if he'd known it was eight-year-olds who'd broken in, he wouldn't have called the cops. I was taken home and given a telling-off by my dad. It was a bit of a shock, my first involvement with the law. But you get over it.

Not that I was regularly involved with the police. That break-in was the first and only offence for a very long time. It wasn't until I went to senior school that I got into trouble like that again. Instead I was using my newly learnt judo skills in any confrontation that came my way. If there was a scuffle at school, if I was being picked on by a taller boy, I'd go for his legs. I'd lift one leg and sweep it along the back. I'd push with my shoulder and all my body weight would go on to him. He'd land on his ribs and lie there winded. Then I'd get him in an armlock and strangle him. That used to stop them picking on me.

But I'd only use my fighting skills to defend myself. I was never a bully, I can say that. I used to sort out the bullies but I'd never, ever bully kids myself. Bullies were scum to me. They used to have their idiots following them around. I wouldn't tolerate them. Even at that age, I'd avoid their company. That kind of behaviour didn't interest me. I was involved in more rebellious things than that outside school, but it never meant picking on weaker people. I was already sure of myself. I knew what I wanted. I think a bully is an insecure person, whatever age they are. As you get older and see and experience more confrontations, you don't need a degree to see why some people are bullies. Having mixed with a number of violent individuals over the years, and having been violent myself, I know why a person behaves like that.

I was always a positive character; that's the family spirit in me. And I was given a very positive home life. My father didn't beat me, so my character was never beaten down. I never needed to think about picking on other people because I didn't feel threatened myself. I was a rebel, a pain in the arse to neighbours and teachers and the local law, but what I did was what other kids were doing at that age. It's just that I did those things too many times. I never thought about it. I was too busy doing it.

From the age of seven or eight, the black guys I used to play with thought I was a complete nutter. They called me 'Bruiser' because I always had a black eye from all the scuffles and fights I was in. From the age of eight up to about twelve years old, I used to read a comic called *The Victor*. I used to buy it every Saturday and was inspired by a character in it called Alf Tupper. Alf would turn up at different sports competitions at short notice and with holes in his trainers, having done his paper round and eaten fish and chips, and still win a race.

I didn't have a hero in the real world. There wasn't anyone I looked up to or idolised, except this comic-strip character. He was probably between twenty-five and thirty-five, and lived in a run-down house. He'd get into scuffles after race meetings and always win the fights. He was rough and ready and I identified with everything about him. Alf was loyal; he had a good heart. He'd help anyone out and he'd take on any sort of challenge. There were so many similarities between us, though I never planned it that way.

One of the turning points in my life came the day my father met another woman and we all moved in together. I was six at the time and it was a real period of adjustment for me, having to adapt to new rules in the home. In fact, I completely rebelled against the situation, although I had to remain there until I was sixteen because the courts had ruled that I had to live with my father. My father and this woman never married, and they split up after falling out. But that was when I was about seventeen or eighteen. So this woman was around during the years when I was getting into scrapes, and she tried to take a disciplinary role. But I always rejected her attempts at authority. The way I saw it, she was trying to mould me into something I was never going to be.

I knew what I wanted to be. The first time I won a judo medal, at the Midlands Junior Championships, I felt great. I must have been about ten at the time. I remember going to the judo club that morning and then on to the centre where the championships were being held. It was a whole new experience, not knowing who I'd be competing against. Afterwards, I remember going round to some of the neighbours and showing them my medal and certificate. I was proud to be a fighter even then.

Shortly after I stopped going to judo at about twelve years old, I went to a boxing club, just to get a taste of the sport. It was Aston Villa Boxing Club, next to the football ground, and it was a fair journey to get to each time. I went along for about a month or so, and I got my nose punched in. It was my opponent's first night there and he meant to wound me. We were only twelve at the time. He cracked my nose and there was blood everywhere. I punched the guy back and made him cry. It was my way of saying, 'Don't come on strong with me, chum, 'cos I can come on strong too.' I didn't care if he cried; he'd made my eyes water and I did the same to him. I suppose, looking at it now, I'd say, 'Don't dish it out if you can't take it,' but you can't verbalise that attitude when you're twelve years old.

I was leading an active life, and getting into trouble was part of it. One minute I was training, next minute I was fighting in the street. Some sports were forced on me. I was never interested in football but it was part of the school curriculum. I played left back because I was good at stopping people when they came forward. I used to tap their legs, not the ball. I was good at knocking people down. They put me near the goal because people couldn't get past me. Better than a goalkeeper. But I never made the school football team. Instead I enjoyed running. I had a real surge of energy, I remember. I'd call out to my dad that I was off for a run, step out and close the front door and come back later.

I'd keep a mental note of the progress I was making. I was devising my own simple training programmes without really thinking about it. I'd say to myself, 'I did that last week, so I can push myself a bit further this week.' I never wrote down what I'd achieved. I knew in my head what I wanted to do.

Already I wanted to be an athlete of some sort. My dad used to watch the boxing on television and I used to watch the matches with him. He also enjoyed athletics and we'd watch the races together. I think watching the athletes on TV inspired me a lot. I used to think, I'd love to do something like that, and then, I could do better than that. Instead of running a hundred metres I wanted to run miles. To me, the hundred-metre races at school were boring. I always wanted to push my body to the extreme. I always wanted to go further. I knew I could do better, maybe not in terms of time but in endurance. I wanted something more physically demanding.

I can remember looking out of a window when I was four or five and living in Minstead Road, and thinking I wanted to do something with my life, be somebody in sport. It was important to come from nothing to something. I've never had any heroes or people I've looked up to during my sporting career. I've probably been too busy studying my own performance. I just got on with it. I'm a role model for others, I'm told, but I didn't look at someone else and say, 'I want to be like him.' At the age of eleven I used to watch the BBC's *Record Breakers* when Roy Castle was presenting it with Norris McWhirter, and I said to myself, 'I want to be on that programme.' When I did get on it, I met both Roy and Norris twice. Lovely bloke, Norris. And I wanted to be in *The Guinness Book of World Records* too.

By the time I got to senior school the teachers had given up on me and let me sit at the back of the class and do what I wanted to do. I was already my own person with my own mindset, and I used to give teachers a mouthful of abuse. They'd let me alone in the end. It didn't bother me if I got told off. I'd just shrug my shoulders and go out for a run. I remember one time we had a football match. I said to the sports teacher, 'I'm not playing football. I'm going out for a run.' And he let me do my own thing. Off I went, doing shuttle sprints, running and press-ups. Shuttle sprints are a good exercise where you sprint between two lines, fifteen metres apart, for explosive power training. This was to help me with my latest interest in boxing.

Dad knew he had a problem with me. And as I got older the incidents multiplied. There was the time he opened the door to a black guy and an Asian, both about my age. They said to him, 'Is Paddy there?' I must have been thirteen or fourteen at the time.

My dad said, 'What do you want to see him for?'

'We want to fight him.'

Dad shouted up to me, 'Patrick, there's some blokes here want to fight you.'

I came down and he told me to go outside with them. He locked the door and stood at the window, watching me.

We started fighting on the grass verge in front of the house. I got the Asian guy in an armlock. He was about three or four inches taller than me, but I was squeezing the hell out of him and I wouldn't let go. I think he'd brought the other guy along for support, because he just stood and watched. We were out there for about ten or fifteen minutes, scuffling and getting a few scrapes. My dad didn't offer to come out and help. He just watched from the window and, when I'd beaten the Asian guy, he opened the door and let me back in. And I went upstairs and washed my face, and that was the end of it.

Once you get into sport and you start looking strong among your peers, you find yourself being challenged. Whether I liked fighting or not, I had to deal with that. From the age of about eight or nine, trouble found me. As I got older I developed a reputation for fighting. Lads dropped round to challenge me. But people get confused between someone who's tough and someone who's crazy and goes up against it. I wasn't crazy really, but I was a hell of a rebel. Being a rebel can mean you're out of control: if there's a rule, you want to break it. Being hard and tough is another thing: you're constantly fighting. As I grew up I was mixing the two elements together, or it was happening to me somehow. I was rebelling and getting into fights all the time. It was as though I was being pulled in two directions at once. I didn't know which way I was going.

After I left school I never went back. I never socialised a lot there, even at senior level, although I'd stop kids being bullied. But I used to keep myself to myself, rather than go around with a group of friends. As for girls, I liked them a lot but I was wedded to my sport even then. To be an athlete, you've got to be focused. That can seem very selfish or self-centred to others, but it's not.

You're being ambitious. Sport is a short-lived career and you've got to take advantage of it while you can.

People may think, He's a selfish basket, he is, and females, especially, can say, 'He's always down the bloody gym.' And during some relationships I had when I was doing sport, I must admit I was mostly down the gym. I still am. But my argument is: I'm bringing money home for my girl and me to go out and have a meal, and to put towards our holiday and to pay the bills. When the money was in the pot, I was generous with it and helped people out. There are two sides to me: I can roll with the punches, but there's a soft side too.

If people want to rumble me, I'll rumble them back, twice as hard. But there's another side: I'd help out, genuinely. I'm not stupid. I can weigh up a situation very fast. I'm a good judge of character. This comes from having a streetwise childhood, being brought up in a working-class family. I can remember getting my clothes from second-hand shops, charity shops like Oxfam. Life was pretty hard but we had a lot of home-made food. When we moved from Minstead Road, after Dad met the other woman, we lived about a mile up the road, in a more well-to-do street where children had a set of parents with regular jobs.

I was like an only child when I was young. My brothers and sisters had all moved on. It might have been one reason I was self-contained: I was always happy to do my own thing at home. Moving schools was a big disruption for me. I went to two junior schools and two senior schools. I'd already had the upheaval of my mother and father splitting up. I went to one junior school for twelve months, then another junior school. Then my father met this lady and we moved again.

I was getting nowhere in the classroom, especially at Jaffray School, my first senior school in Erdington. It was a multicultural comprehensive; a lot of black kids went there. I was there for a couple of years, from 1976 to 1978, and I was always in trouble, fighting with the troublemakers. They should have put us in the gym, put some boxing gloves on us and let us sort it out.

One day I was picked on by a black guy. I've got a lot of black friends and I love West Indian food, and this guy, Joseph Harris, is a lovely guy now. He's turned out well and we both do karate, but he had a loud mouth at school and he picked on me. He kept pushing me in the dinner hall. Afterwards, in the playground, I automatically got him in a judo hold, a *tomanagi*, and threw him over me. I'd stopped doing judo by then, but you don't forget the things you learn at an early age. He went flying through the air like a rocket and landed on the concrete, on his head and shoulders.

All of a sudden I'm in the headmaster's office again, getting the cane. Six of the best. And I'm thinking, Well, I never started this. But the other boy got the cane, as well. I've seen him since and he said to me, 'I remember the time you rag-dolled me.'

I said, 'Well, you deserved it.' We laughed about it. He's a black belt in karate now and we're the best of friends.

And, lo and behold, I found myself fighting his cousin, Winston 'Spider' Harris, in a European Record Full Contact Fighters Combat title fight in August 1995. In that competition I fought different boxers in five hundred and sixty rounds over a period of a month. Winston is a lovely guy, like Joseph, and he's been British Kickboxing Champion seven times. So I fought and beat one family member in the playground, and fought and beat one in the ring.

Often I meet up with people I fought at school. We say hello and talk professionally and laugh about past confrontations. We were kids then, and you grow up. If you're a man of the world you do the business and defend yourself, and you don't have to think about it for the rest of your life. You laugh about it; that's what men are all about. I've never been one for picking up a knife or a gun. It's not my style. It was always bare-knuckle fighting out in the playground.

CHAPTER 3

ROLLING WITH THE PUNCHES

I STOPPED GOING to judo with my cousins when I changed schools at eleven. I was small and stocky and always fighting people who were bigger than me, often in David and Goliath situations. Not long after I got to senior school, I started getting a name for myself as a bit of a rebel. The lads wanted to sort me out. All the violence escalated from there really.

I was often marched into the headmaster's office, asked about my offence and caned, usually six times on the hand. I just accepted it. One time I remember, I didn't do my science homework and I got the slipper, again about six times. But I wasn't interested in science or any other homework. Sport was the only part of school life that counted for me. I'd already got a bit of a reputation at my primary school, and some of the boys who'd been there went on to Jaffray School with me. Jaffray had a bad reputation, anyway, as far as education and discipline were concerned. It wasn't the best of schools, but there I was. I think my father regretted that I'd gone there, but he never said anything about it. We weren't great communicators about subjects like that. Conversation was minimal, although it was never unpleasant or hostile. Dad looked after me well.

It was when I was about twelve that I started to take sports seriously. We were doing different sports at school, such as gymnastics, and we were encouraged to develop our athletic skills. Trampolining was something I enjoyed: the buzz of jumping up and down and doing back flips; the skill of it. Trampoline work is about strength and flexibility and focusing on a centre line. It's about balance and technique, co-ordination and combination. I didn't think I was any good at the sport but I was selected to represent the school.

We went along to Castle Vale Senior School for the area heat of the Midlands Schools Championships. The event covered the north of Birmingham. In the competition, you had two minutes each to demonstrate your skill and versatility, just as you do in other gymnastic competitions. If I got through that, it would get tough because the finals would place take in Greater Manchester. Well, I got through to the finals at Washwood Heath School, and I got a bronze medal at the Midland Schools Championships.

I also represented the school in athletics in 1977 and 1978, when I was thirteen and fourteen, in the fifteen hundred metres and the long jump. At my primary school, sports had been organised as team games; athletics wasn't encouraged as much as football. At senior school, athletics, a sport for individuals, was more to the fore and that appealed to me. I found that in team games I kept arguing with people about whose fault it was when something went wrong. I hated that. I just wanted to get on with the job. I've always been like that.

But I had to put a lot more time in for training, especially after school. As you got bigger, the competition grew harder. I didn't always win. Then I'd feel disappointed and frustrated. I always felt I could have done better. I told myself I had to work harder. But the PT teachers at Jaffray encouraged and motivated me. They wanted me to do well. They saw I had potential and that was job satisfaction for them. Jaffray may have been a rough school, but it had a reputation for success in sports.

I played soccer for the school, even though I'm not naturally a team player; I must have been doing something right. We were in the Midland Schools Championships, so I must have had some ability. But I was never a keen watcher of football. I was much more interested in boxing and the martial arts. The martial arts include ju-jitsu and tai-kwando, and there's a new category called freestyle martial arts, which is a combination of judo, tai-kwando and karate. Judo involves a lot of groundwork, while ju-jitsu is more about grappling and holding and throwing. Karate is punching and kicking. Tai-kwando is a combination of punching and kicking, similar to karate, and is an Olympic sport now. I enjoy karate and still go to a club around the corner and train with senior instructors.

When I was at school, all my friends would be going out to play in the evenings and weekends but, if I wasn't training, I'd go off for a run. It might only have been a mile run, but it seemed like ten miles at that age when my body was still undersized. My dad would say, 'Where are you going now, Patrick?' And I'd say, 'Off for a run, Dad.' He couldn't understand it. And I'd be doing press-ups at home, upstairs in my bedroom. I hadn't read about training in a book, I just enjoyed doing it. I was so full of energy. And I felt I had something to prove to myself. I was going in two directions at once: there was the sport and there was the violence. I had so much energy that I was looking in every direction for an outlet.

When I was twelve I joined the Royal Engineers Army Cadets at their Erdington branch. This was an evening activity, separate from school. I think it was a school friend who mentioned it to me, so I went along to their Nissen hut and applied to join. The boys there were aged between twelve and sixteen. We did marching drill and army cadet exercises and went away to military camp. They soon saw my aptitude for sport. Next thing, I was representing them in cross-country running and won a couple of medals, including a team competition at Sutton Park. It was a Midlands Army Cadet Championship, and there were about a hundred other competitors. We entered as a team of four and came away with the gold medal.

I was over the moon when we won that medal, even in the disciplined structure of a team effort. With cross-country, you still have to run as an individual, even though you collect points for the team. You don't run at the same pace as anyone else; you still go out there and bust a gut for two or three miles. I was never a particularly fast runner over short distances, but I'd overtake the sprinters on a longer course. Even then, I realised I was best at endurance events.

The army cadets come under the umbrella of the Territorial Army, the TA. The cadets were set up to encourage young people to join the military later on. It's different from your Boys' Brigade or the Scouts; it's more disciplined. You'd have a fourteen-year-old cadet corporal telling you what to do. And I accepted the discipline. I thought it was great. I thoroughly enjoyed myself and stayed on for two and half years, until I changed school.

Unlike at school, in the cadets I felt I was being encouraged to do something. It was different thinking. At school I wasn't encouraged in subjects I was weak in. And if you're not encouraged, you lose interest. We're all human. Everyone needs to be motivated with a pat on the back, whoever they are.

But one day I gave the sports master a lot of cheek. He whacked me so hard around the ear that it got infected. At fourteen and a half, after two and a half years of fighting in the playground and getting the cane, I was sent to another comprehensive, a Roman Catholic school called Saint Edmund Campion. I'm a Catholic but not a practising one.

My new school, also in Erdington, didn't inspire me sportswise. I didn't represent it in any sports. The sports teachers at Jaffray had encouraged me to enter competitions. They hadn't pushed me into anything but they'd encouraged me to do what I wanted to do. This new school lacked the kind of PT instructors I needed. Jaffray had been a rougher school, but it shone in sports and that had motivated me. This school was nowhere in the school football league. So I lost interest and did my own thing.

The violence started to escalate after that. It was around this age that I had my first street fight. It was one street gang against another. Lads of about eighteen were fighting other young lads. It was gang warfare in Erdington High Street and the surrounding area. I was fourteen and getting stuck in and loving it.

In one particular fight, I remember, a guy went to punch me. I kicked him and he went down. That's what street fights are: anything goes. There are no rules. These fights aren't planned. And this one just happened that night. The other gang hated the guys I was with, and the fighting developed from that. I was part of one gang and it wouldn't have occurred to me to stop and think whether it was anything to do with me. They weren't even friends of mine, but I stood by them. It's being part of a gang. I followed it through. It was teamwork, but I really enjoyed the aggression.

At the time I was mostly running on my own and doing exercises at home in my bedroom. It was personal choice. I'd go for a run around the local streets and do press-ups and sit-ups at home. I concentrated on strength and stamina exercises, seeing how much I could do, how far I could push myself in a certain time. If I did one hundred press-ups one day, I'd go for double the next. I enjoyed seeing myself improve and kept a record in my head of how I was progressing. I felt stronger and more confident in myself and I ended up with a high level of stamina and fitness. And this was to stand me in good stead later on.

I wasn't ever really a smoker. I'd tried smoking at school, but the thing I was best at was coughing up my guts after a ciggy. I was just experimenting with fags; you had to follow the crowd. I smoked because everyone else did, but not much. My lungs stayed clear. They got decoked every time I ran down the street. Self-discipline came naturally to me. I was happy to run and run. I wore the usual trainers and tracksuit bottoms or shorts. I didn't keep track of how many miles I was doing; I just headed out and came back.

I don't know if anyone else was running around that area. I think I was thought of as a bit of a head case. They'd call me 'crazy' or 'Mad Paddy' or 'Paddy Whack'. But, although I was still a rebel at school, I'd also started to become a bit of a peacemaker. I used to pick on the school bullies who picked on the weak kids.

A nice thing happened to me about seven or eight years ago. I was out shopping one day and a guy came up to me. He said, 'Paddy, you don't remember me, do you?' I told him I didn't and he said, 'You used to stop me getting bullied at school. You used to step in and stop the bullying. I just want to thank you for it.' I thought it was great that he remembered that.

There was always at least one cock of the yard strutting about the playground. They were the big guys and they could see I was becoming a fighter. One day I went up to one of them on the school stairway and offered to see him outside. He declined the invitation, even though he was bigger than me. And I noticed he was shaking. We were both about fourteen or fifteen, but he was nudging six foot. I was a lot shorter, about five foot seven. He always had three or four boys going around with him. I'd noticed him kicking people and taking their money. He reckoned he could pick on others, but I decided, that day, I'd had enough of watching it.

I approached him on the stairs. Even then, I made sure he was above me, standing a couple of steps higher with his group of hangers-on. 'You think you're hard,' I said. 'You think you're a bully. Let's go outside and sort it out.'

'I don't want to fight you, Paddy, he said.'

But I put pressure on him. 'Let's go for it now, out in the playground,' I said. 'Me and you, right now.' But he wouldn't. His face was going red and I could see him gulping saliva. He walked away in front of his own team, and he lost his status. After that most of the bullying stopped. Others had seen that moment of confrontation and one or two of his followers dropped away.

It just seemed to be a natural progression, on my way to other things. It was me sorting things into the right order, stopping the weaker ones being picked on. I wasn't having it. This gang leader went around in a group. He always needed the gang to support him. I was an individualist. I was happy to bide my time.

This is what makes people wary of me, even now. The tamped-up aggression was always there, latent. I could wait my moment. I've seen that guy a lot since school. He still fancies himself. Not with me, but within his own little bubble. He still lives in the same area, but get him out of that place and he's a nobody. I know how to deal with individuals like that.

One of the members of his gang, an Asian lad, was also a bully. He kept having a go at me, saying, 'If you have a go at him, have a go at me too.' I've nothing against Asians; plenty of them come to my gym. But one day this guy was having a go at a girl in the classroom, then having a go at another lad who tried to intervene. I got up on the desk and punched him in the head. Next thing, he was on the floor, bleeding. He started crying and I said, 'You're not going to bully again, are you?' I can't stand bullying. I really hate it. We were fifteen then, in our last year at school. You'd think the guy would have had more sense. But he hadn't. I didn't go around in a gang. I used to walk out of school on my own. I didn't need hangers-on.

By this time I was starting to get into trouble with the police. I didn't start playing truant until I was about fifteen but, if it hadn't been for my interest in sport, I would have been heading for prison by then. My energy would have been translated into violence. I was heading in that direction.

I remember one of our school discos, where a gang from another school turned up. They started throwing bricks and stones at us as we came out of the disco. There were more of them than us, but I said to the lads, 'Let's go for it,' and we ran after the gang, down the street. I was up front, leading the chase, and I picked up a scaffolding bar that was lying on the ground nearby. It was a handy tool for deflecting bricks and stones and I ran across the road with it, straight towards the other gang. But, as I tore round a corner, I ran straight into a police officer. I dropped the bar immediately. I'd only wielded it to show the other gang I'd got something to fight with too. But, if the teachers weren't clouting me, the police were. I got a good clip round the ear from the copper, which probably did me good. He gave me a real telling-off. He cautioned me and told me to move on.

But one or two of the lads who were supposed to be with us while we were chasing the gang had, in fact, chickened out. I went back and got hold of one of them who'd lost his bottle and threw him over a garden fence. My reasoning was he should have stood by us. We needed him. It wasn't the moment for him to think of us being outnumbered, twenty to four. He'd wanted to go home, so I had to do some brainstorming on him. I struck him. I didn't know what I was doing, I was that angry. I've seen him once or twice since then. He still lives in the area. I presume he's forgotten about what I did but he still looks at me warily.

I must have been about sixteen then. I didn't know, for sure, what I was going to do with my life or how it was going to pan out, but I was getting some idea of what I wanted to do. I'd already got visions of doing my own thing in some way, and I was now looking for a more aggressive contact sport than judo.

I was getting into a lot of trouble around this time and a friend suggested I take up boxing. I missed going to the judo club but I wanted a new challenge. I thought I had another skill in a different area. It's hard for a lot of people to make the change from the martial arts to boxing; not everyone can do it. But I had the ability to adapt to a different discipline and I'd already had a taste of boxing at Aston

Villa when I was twelve. This time I joined the Austin Amateur Boxing Club at Longbridge, where they made the cars.

For a while boxing absorbed all my troublemaker's aggression. I concentrated on getting into the ring, sparring and doing punchbag work and I focused on preparing for competitions and tournaments. A lot of people will tell you they've boxed, but punching a bag and getting into the ring are two different things. There's nothing like the real thing.

I enjoyed the fighting. I was still pumped full of aggression, everyone could see that. I was wild, even in the ring. I was like a windmill, arms and legs going all the time. I was always going forwards, coming at people. I realised I was a pressure fighter, constantly in the face of my opponent, regardless of how often or how hard I got hit. I was on top of them all the time. That's pure aggression.

I spent about a year and a half in the gym, learning boxing skills. Then, in 1983, when I was nineteen, I had my first fight. I was never a boxer; I was always a fighter. A boxer takes his time and picks his punches. A pressure fighter just goes forward, all hell let loose. I'd been told to stand back and pick my moment, but I never did. I stuck to my own style of fighting, which probably lost me my first fight as an amateur boxer. I kept coming forward.

I'd already had my nose broken at the Aston Villa club but it was to happen again in my first amateur boxing tournament as a welterweight in 1983. I was a novice fighting a tall, black guy from another boxing club. I'd looked at him in the changing room before the match, and I thought, He's too big and tall for me. I wondered if they'd weighed us properly. But I'm very heavy-boned and stocky in build. Out we went, into the ring. All my friends were there to support me, thinking I was going to do well. The place – I think it was a social club – was packed out with about three or four hundred people. In the second round I felt my nose go. And I heard the crowd say, 'Oooh!' They'd heard the snap.

Then I got the guy with a left hook. I nearly had him. He was wobbly; I could see his feet going. But the referee stopped the fight because, by this time, blood was pouring out of my nose. I don't know whose side the ref was on. I was still fighting, and I was even starting to beat the guy, but the match was stopped. It was a clean break to the nose but there was blood all over my face and I was swallowing it. They couldn't stop the flow of it and if you have a gum shield in, it restricts the breathing. So they stopped the fight.

They're very strict in amateur boxing about this kind of situation because of the possibility of head injuries and fatalities. At that time, as an amateur, you didn't have to wear a head guard. There was no law about wearing them. And there I was, coming forward all the time, just as I did when I was sparring.

I heard that the other guy stopped fighting one or two fights after that. Boxing's a hard game. After he beat me, I heard he lost the next fight and couldn't take the defeat. To be a good sportsman, an athlete and a champion, you've got to accept the losing side of the coin. It's hard, but, in every sense, you've got to roll with punches.

Once I'd got my first two fights out of the way, I was on a

winning streak. I'd learnt the hard way to take my time and listen to what they told me in my corner. And I started to listen to other people in the gym. I hadn't done that before. I'd always thought I was right. Now I was maturing and starting to think. I wanted to be more than pure brawn. I stopped relying on my aggression. I realised there were skilful people out there who worked harder at techniques and, as a result, were better at the sport than I was.

When it came to my third fight, I altered my game plan and started winning. This fight was with a boxer who'd had about twelve or fourteen fights. I was well outmatched. He was with the Bugle Horn Boxing Club at Northfield, in the south-west of Birmingham. It's closed down now. But the guy had all his friends and family and supporters there. The hall was packed with three hundred people. My only supporters were my two corner men from my gym, who were also my club trainers, and my brother and sister. I could hear the shouts all around me: 'You Irish bastard!' and other insults. In fact, I was born and bred in England and I've got the British flag on one of the shelves for my trophies.

It was my twenty-first birthday that night. I went in there and I beat the guy on points. It was a unanimous decision. I remember my hand being raised and the crowd still booing me because their golden boy hadn't won. He'd been winning fights up till then and his friends probably had money on him that night. I headed for the changing rooms and the crowd who'd been booing a few minutes before cleared a path for me, because I'd proved I was the best. I looked at one or two of them as I went by, as if to say, 'Call me a name now, then?' They were a typical lager-lout crowd. But when I walked back through the middle of them, everything went silent. And my brother and sister were proud of me.

*   *   *

I'd left the army cadets when I changed school at around fourteen and a half. By the time I was sixteen I'd started thinking about what I wanted to do with the rest of my life. And I thought, again, of the army. The careers officers came to the school in our last year to advise all the school leavers about future careers. From school I joined the Junior Parachute Regiment, which is a regular boys' service of the armed forces. And I didn't have to work at getting fit for the exercises and courses; I'd already done that.

Browning Barracks in Aldershot, Hampshire, was the depot of the Parachute Regiment. It was a new part of the world for me. We were treated like juniors, like boys. I disliked that intensely. It was like school to me and I wanted to be treated like a man. I wanted to be at the senior level of the services. But my brother, who'd been in the Royal Artillery for about six years, warned me this was how it would be. He'd told me I wouldn't like it, and he was right. He'd got a ranking and advised me to wait until I was older before I joined up. He knew what the Junior Paras would be like. But I couldn't wait. And I made a mistake.

We did the usual weapons training, navigational skills, camping and assault course work. The point of the junior service is to build you up for the men's army. They try to increase your stamina and your confidence. We learnt to use the SLR, the self-loading rifle,

44

and the GPMG, the general-purpose machine gun, which fires four hundred rounds a minute.

I noticed I was fitter than the blokes around me. I'd be first going over the assault courses and finishing the cross-country runs – unless I had flu or was suffering from an injury that day, and then I'd come third or fourth or fifth. I was thin and wiry then. I was muscular but agile. I could move like a whippet. In the BFTs, the Battle Fitness Tests, I came first. In the armed forces you have to pass fitness tests every year. They have to make sure you're up to the job.

I can't say I made any friends there. At the junior level, people come and go. The real problem was, I thought I was missing out on something. At sixteen I felt I should have been down the pub and having girlfriends, instead of square-bashing. But I was a good lad in the junior army, unlike my later army experiences. At that age I was as keen as mustard. It was a new environment and I was doing well, but I decided to leave. They tried to persuade me to stay. They could see potential in me. My section commander, a ginger-haired lance corporal called Betts, was a nice bloke and did his best to change my mind.

We were allowed out at night, under supervision. But we weren't allowed into pubs because we were under age. The military police in Aldershot were very strict. If you didn't have your ID card on you, it was an immediate fine. They'd put you in prison for offences and I don't think they'd hesitate to use a baton. The military are like a law unto themselves. They'll deal with you in the way they see fit, and you've got to go along with it. If the civilian police found you messing about in Aldershot, they'd get shot of you to the military police. They knew you'd get dealt with properly. If a civilian policeman hit you with a baton or manhandled you, you could have him. The military police must have some arrangement that encourages the law to hand you over to them – fast.

Other evenings were spent getting ready for inspection, cleaning our kit. We had to polish our boots and do our washing and ironing. Everyone had a room job, a specific job within your block, cleaning the toilets or whatever, and the job had to be done. It was an experience in itself but, at sixteen, you don't want to know about it. I stuck that life for six months, then applied to come out. Army life could be enjoyable but I kept asking myself, 'What else am I missing?' I wanted to have my cake and eat it. I wanted to go out with my mates *and* be in the army. But you can't do both. For that very reason there was a large turnover of juniors: about forty per cent. I wasn't the only one who missed his freedom. Four or five lads left the same day as I did. My mum was pleased to see me.

CHAPTER 4

HEADBANGER

I HAD AN IDEA I'd go back into the army later on. But, just then, I wanted to live life. I was eighteen when I learnt to drive, but each driving instructor I had passed me on to another one. They didn't like the way I kept putting my foot down on the accelerator. During one lesson we drove over some hills, a great walking and driving spot, and I decided to put my foot down. I was yelling like a cowboy, 'Yahoo!', as I speeded along.

All I could hear was the voice of the instructor shouting, 'Slow down! Slow down!'

And I shouted back, 'Ah, shuddup! What's the matter with you? I gotta have some fun!'

When I turned up for my lesson the following week, I found the instructor had sent his brother along instead. He took me out for my lesson and, again, I was a bit courageous and put my foot down. At the end of the lesson the brother told me I'd have another instructor the following week. It turned out to be a different driving school altogether. That's how far they'd passed me on. Washed their hands of me.

I was given a few more lessons, this time by a female instructor, and I drove fairly carefully. Then I moved house, to Quinton, another district in Birmingham, and started with another school of motoring. After numerous lessons with a new instructor, my driving improved. I applied for a test and failed it, and put in for another one. As usual, we went for the hourly drive around the area before the test. I looked across at the guy and saw he was drinking cans of super-strength lager. He was an alcoholic and had a load of cans under his seat. He wanted to go for a drink with me after the test. I just wanted him to drop me off, as fast as possible. But he must have brought me luck because I passed my driving test that day.

When I came back from the Junior Paras, I moved from my father's to my mother's house. I was sixteen and a half at the time, and I soon got a local job, working in Tesco, pushing trolleys, stacking shelves and helping out with security. The area where the supermarket was situated, near Ladywood in Edgbaston, had a high rate of crime and they needed help looking out for shoplifters. A lot of alcoholics and drug addicts used to come in and shoplift. You never knew what these people were carrying. They'd use bottles if they were approached, to make good their escape. I wasn't hired to be part of security personnel but I was happy to help when assistance was needed.

At the time it was the commissionaires who were in charge of security. These were fairly elderly gentlemen, ex-forces. I respected those guys. I said to them, 'If you get any problems, I'll help you out.' And sometimes they did need assistance. If I saw them trying to restrain a violent shoplifter, I'd run to their aid.

One incident happened, not in the shop itself, but in the car park next to the store. A guy there was caught looking at cars and the police were called. I could see the police in a scuffle with this young lad. A police officer was on top of him. I ran out to see what was going on. But I was in two minds whether to help or not.

It was a moment of divided loyalties. I was a lad who'd come from nothing. I wasn't sure whether I was with the policeman or the guy who'd got caught. I had to stop in my tracks. I couldn't help out. The police officer looked at me. Our eyes met. He understood. He said to me, 'Don't even think about it. Don't you come near me.' That was the turning point. I didn't help out. I did nothing at all. Just stood there. I was at some kind of crossroads, staring down two paths. If I'd helped the potential thief, then I don't know which of those paths I'd have taken.

After that, I started to get my act together. Now, if I saw a police officer getting beaten up, I'd help him straight away. But at that age you don't know the direction you're travelling in. You're still finding your feet. And I'd had run-ins with the law myself. They weren't my best friends at the time.

But that was it: a subtle change of direction. It went undetected by me at the time. I carried on at Tesco for another twelve months but I began falling out with the management, having disagreements with them. I was seen as a bit of a headbanger, a rebel. That was how I was projecting myself, and it was causing me problems. Not that I got the sack from the job. What happened was I was called into the office one day. I'd been having disagreements with other members of staff and they were getting weary of me. I'd be picking fights with the men downstairs in the warehouse. I was a complete tearaway. If I disagreed with someone, I'd say, 'Right, I'll fight you.'

Some fellow would make a remark, and I'd make one back and it would escalate from there. I wouldn't react in that way now; I'm too mature. But then, I'd say, 'I'll fight you now.' I had a lot of anger and aggression inside me, always about to explode. Maybe it was to do with one or two bad patches in my childhood which had left a certain amount of bitterness. I hadn't got on with my father's woman friend. There'd been ups and downs at home.

Tesco realised they had a problem with me. The final straw was when I offered to fight one of the butchers in the store. He already had a large butcher's knife in his hand, but I said, 'I'll still fight you with that.' I didn't care what the guy had in his hand. He wouldn't fight me. He probably went straight to the manager. Someone did.

The manager called me into his office and said, 'Paddy, we'd like you to leave. We'll give you a good reference and two months' money.' And they did. Tesco stood by me, but they didn't want any more of my kind of trouble. I got another job, part-time, in another supermarket closer to home, just to bring the money in. I was there seven or eight months and I started working as a doorman in the evenings.

I was introduced to the evening work by a friend of mine. He was already 'on the doors'. I started off by working with him in a couple of pub discos, then I graduated from there. At first I was freelance, looking after DJs. The club manager would ask us to come in. Pub discos have a lot more trouble than nightclubs. Dress is more casual; it's a local venue and the people wear jeans. Families drink in there, and there's sometimes confrontations between families. In that situation you're not just a doorman, you're a social worker trying to calm down the warring factions. It was a good training ground for me.

I started out doing the doors for the Talbot in Hagley Road, Birmingham, and the Duke of York at Harborne. After a while I gave up the supermarket work and only worked at night. Then I got a job at Snobs nightclub, near Broad Street, in the centre of Birmingham. There were a lot of youths there between the ages of about eighteen and twenty-four. It wasn't a nightclub with a mature clientele, so there was trouble regularly.

One night we refused to let a football team into the club. They started smashing the front windows and kicking in the front door while we stood there, trying to contain the situation. Another time things got out of hand downstairs. A group of lads were getting boisterous. I went down there, thinking I had the back-up of the other four or five doormen. But they'd disappeared; all happened to go to the toilet at the same time. I was the shortest guy there and I had to go in on my own. Well, I used my head to sort out the fracas, and it paid off. But I didn't work for that club again. Those doormen had lost their bottle. They'd let me down.

Around that time I'd been going for lads' nights out with the guys from Tesco and getting into scrapes and fights, with doormen and other gangs of youths around the city centre. We'd go to clubs and pubs and, after a few drinks, we'd be creating trouble.

On one occasion we went for a night out, starting at the Crooked House in Dudley. The Crooked House is an old pub on the slant, like the Leaning Tower of Pisa. You go inside and the bars are on the slant. We had a drink in there, then we went back into the centre of Dudley and found a pub disco. There were about four of us. Some guys in the disco were taking the mickey out of us, so I said to them, 'Well, come outside and look at my car.' They fell for it. They followed me and, as they stood looking at my car, I struck out. There were four of them and I hit two. They'd been getting aggressive inside the disco, but I didn't want to start a confrontation in there. I wanted to ask them what it was all about outside. My friends came along with me, but I did the fighting. They stood by, shocked. Like the mickey-takers, they'd believed I'd actually wanted to sell my car. We left them there and drove off.

Looking back, I do regret some of the incidents I instigated. I was far from perfect, I'll be honest. I was a young man, full of aggression. I started confrontations unnecessarily. I looked for trouble then. I'm a different person now. From about seventeen to twenty-one I was known as a troublemaker, especially by doormen of pubs and clubs. I was banned from a lot of the clubs in Birmingham for a very long time. I was a problem for the club owners. I had a lot of rage in me. I'd drink and cause fights. Once or twice I even knocked out doormen.

When I was about nineteen, I was in Horts Wine Bar in Edgbaston. I was with a friend and we were talking to a girl, not realising that the girl was going out with the doorman. He was a giant of a man: about six foot three. We were pleasant to the girl and we didn't think anything more about it. We were going through the door when the man threatened me for talking to his girlfriend. I apologised and said I didn't realise she was with him. But he got aggressive, so I hit him. I only weighed about nine and a half or ten stone but I knocked him out.

I didn't plan it. It was only when he went over the boundary of normal threatening noises that I reckoned I'd have to do something. I looked at our difference in height and struck him on the jaw, punching upwards. He was on his back. He dropped like a sack of spuds.

But I reckoned I was in the right. I'd apologised to him. I'd told him I wasn't aware the girl was his girlfriend. But the guy came forward and wanted to carry on the argument in front of a group of people, including his girlfriend, so I had to think quickly. But I didn't realise a friend of the gaffer of Horts was talking to the doorman at the time, trying to calm down the situation. I told the gaffer the other guy had started it, but we still had to leave. We walked off to the car and disappeared.

Twelve months later we were in the same wine bar. I'd been to the gym, then gone on to the wine bar with a friend of mine. We shared a bottle of wine and I'd had nothing to eat, so I got drunk. I went to the toilet and there were two giant blokes in there. I kept thinking I was going to get mugged and I'd better do something. So I hit the two of them. I was wild in those days. I just hit them against the wall. I walked out and rejoined my friend. Next birthday he got me a T-shirt which had on it 'Paddy Doyle Giant Killer'.

The doorman at Horts knew us and he couldn't stop laughing. He made a joke out of the incident. He kept saying, 'It's good here, isn't it?' But I had to leave. I went home with my friend and, when we got to his house, he left me in the car because I was so drunk. He thought I'd sleep it off. When I came to, I didn't know where I was. I kicked all his windows in, trying to get out. I completely wrecked the car. Kicked his door through. I was crazy; I didn't know what I was doing. I only knew I wanted to get out of the vehicle.

During those three or four years I was in a bubble of my own: a total headbanging rage. I used to go out with my mates, not to find a girl but to have a confrontation. If I woke up on a Sunday morning and I hadn't had a fight the night before, I reckoned it had been a bad night. I didn't need drink to fire me up. I've never needed drink like a drug. But drink was acid to me.

And I was hanging around with blokes who were older than me, in their late twenties and early thirties. They were a load of crooks and villains and they could see the potential in me. They took me on board and led me in their direction. And I admit I was happy to go that way for a period of time.

I was never involved with drugs. I was never a thief. But I was involved in violence. Because I was a headbanger, people would see me as the right person to sort out problems. I'd get money for it. Businessmen would ring me up and say, 'Sort this out for me,

Paddy. There's this amount of money in it for you.' So I'd go and scare the people.

As I got older I was veering towards being part of the heavy mob. I had a reputation, even at nineteen and twenty. I was doing the doors at clubs and discos, but other doormen were wary of me. They were established hard men and I was still a youth. They'd take one look at me and they knew I was a problem. Once one doorman knows about you, they all know. Even when I went into the regular army, the Paras, later on, I was coming home on leave and getting a reputation.

I also began to get seriously interested in amateur boxing around that time. The sport helped me find my feet. It channelled my aggression. I wanted to develop my strength, so I decided to take up weight training. There were a number of gyms in Birmingham, but word gets around about which are the best and I went to a reputable club called the Harborne Weight Training Centre, which was owned and run by a guy called Ralph Farqharson.

I was doing gym work, amateur boxing and weight training, all at the same time, and the last gave me added strength. Ralph Farqharson became my trainer. He'd been the World Masters Power Lifting Champion and had a *Guinness Book of World Records* title for beer-barrel lifting. Unfortunately the record was broken after a couple of months by a Swedish strong man. But Ralph was to become a good friend.

Ralph set about showing me the techniques for lifting and I was glad to learn from a champion. He has two gyms: the Harborne

Weight Training Centre, where I trained, and another weightlifting gym in Tyseley, which is also in Birmingham. I still see him and his wife, Sharon. Lovely couple. Genuine people too. Down-to-earth, working-class people who've worked their way up.

Ralph began coaching me on the weights, which gave greater power to my fighting ability. He taught me the technique for lifting: bend the knees, flat back and head up. Never lift anything up with your legs straight. And only lift the weights you're comfortable lifting. I began experimenting with my body, pushing it to its limits. I enjoy weightlifting, but it became obvious that I was doing too much of it at the time. I had muscle, so I had strength, but not flexibility. I was training as much as a weightlifter does, not as a boxer or an athlete. That was ignorance on my part, wanting to go the extra mile. The result was I increased my body mass and that made me less agile in the ring.

I'd always loved boxing, even just sparring in the gym. But I loved getting into the ring and fighting properly. There's nothing like the real thing. At first I worked in Tesco during the day and did my weight training and boxing in the evening. I'd get the train straight after work to the boxing club or to the gym. Practically every night I was somewhere, doing sport. And Friday night I was out with the lads.

I had kept up the boxing for about four years. I was seventeen and working on the doors by then. Being a doorman, you could see where I was going: in the direction of the heavies, the guys who were the gangsters. Doormen and bouncers are hard men, good to have on your side. There I was, a seventeen-year-old, and trying to stop grown men coming in the pub, drunk. It was hard work.

I remember one pub I was working in, where a guy took a knife out. I didn't have any fear. I stepped in between him and the guy he was threatening. I took the knife away from him and threw him out. Fear just wasn't there when I was young. I'd rather have died than lost a confrontation, as demonstrated a decade or so later when I was stabbed in the leg.

I'd never got beaten up in the playground at school, thank God, but when I was about twenty I got beaten in a gang fight. We were outnumbered. There were three of us at a club in the centre of Birmingham. We were completely set up by a large gang of lads, about a dozen of them. At first we didn't know what was going on. Two of my friends had chairs land on them from over a table and I got jumped on from behind. I was punched and kicked around the floor. Unfortunately I'd had a few beers and I didn't know what was going on. I lost my two bottom teeth. I felt them go, felt the crunch. I was attacked from behind and, as I was being pulled back, someone must have thrown a punch or an object at me. I was dragged on to the floor, but I kept fighting.

After that, all I remember was getting up off the floor, eyes turning black and blood pouring from my mouth. I went over to collect the other two lads, who'd been knocked cold with the chairs. One of them was still out, snoring. He wasn't cut but he had a hell of a lump. I pushed the other guys off him, just as another chair was about to rain down on his head. It could have been the final blow to a delicate part of his skull. I got him on his feet and dragged him out of the door. I wasn't going anywhere without my mate. It was loyalty. We may have been outnumbered, we may have been beaten, but you don't leave without taking your casualties with you.

I'd always intended to go back into the Paras. I didn't see much future for me in door work. I was coming up to twenty-one when I applied to join the Parachute Regiment. By the time I'd won my first amateur boxing competition, I'd been through the army's selection procedure and their interviews and was ready to join up. I think the selection process was a lot harder than it is today. The whole process takes three or four months. There are the usual police checks and they take up references. It costs thousands of pounds to train a soldier, so the army has to protect its investment as best it can. They have to be sure you're the right man for the job, as far as possible.

I joined the Paras because I knew it would be tough and demanding. I wanted that challenge. It appealed to my aggressive nature, my determined nature. In March 1984 I was back at Browning Barracks, where for the first six months I was just a recruit. One hundred of us joined at the same time. Six months later seventy of the lads had left or failed the recruitment. Only thirty of us got through.

I could see the numbers in our block dwindling day by day. Men were missing their families, missing their girls. What I'd gone through at sixteen when I'd joined the Junior Paras, they were going through at the age of twenty-one plus. What I'd thought I was missing out on four years earlier, they thought they were missing then. They must have been leading a boring life up to then. Me, I'd lived a bit. I'd got the mad nights with my mates out of my system. Or so I thought.

CHAPTER 5

THE RED BERET

MY FELLOW RECRUITS ranged in age from eighteen to twenty-eight, but I was more streetwise than a lot of them. I'd been there and done it. Which was just as well. Life in the Parachute Regiment was tough: a lot of bullying and beasting went on. Beasting means you're made to do extra physical fitness exercises to the extreme. You go through various fitness tests anyway when you arrive, so the army can see what level you're at and, most likely, get to work on you.

From there you follow the normal recruit training programme leading to selection. Being a recruit doesn't automatically make you a paratrooper. You've got to get through those six months first. You can fail on the fifth month through injury. Fitness and aggression are what the Paras work on, and this did me a lot of good. I also had some excellent training officers. They had high standards. My section commander was a bloke called Corporal Croft. He demanded a high level of discipline, fitness and hygiene. He was a perfectionist, and I had a great deal of respect for him. I learnt a lot from him while I was a recruit.

We were billeted in a massive three-storey modern block. There were eight lads in my room to start with. By the end of the recruitment period, seven had gone. I was the only one left, so I was put in another room. The way the army see it, a recruit who's thinking about leaving is bad for general morale. Everyone else will want to leave. It can spread like a plague, so they get rid of fading recruits fast. If someone wants to leave in the early stages, they're allowed to. This mostly happens in the first couple of months. Even in the fourth month there are lads who've had enough or are getting medically discharged.

The regime is physically very demanding. To survive is to win, as they say. Anything could happen to you during that period: physical injury or mental injury or a family crisis back home. In the Paras they push you to the limit and you've got to learn how to take it. I remember, towards the end of my six months of training, just before I got my red beret and parachute wings, I made a mistake during the drill for the passing-out parade. For that, the corporal punched me in the back of the head. And, just because I flinched and moved my shoulders, he sent me to jail for a couple of hours to be beasted.

They put me in a cell and I was ordered to take my shirt off. Then they made me do physical fitness exercises without a break for the period I was in there. Non-stop press-ups, non-stop circuit training exercises. And I did them without stopping until the Regimental Military Police got sick and tired of looking at me.

'Haven't you had enough?' they asked.

'No,' I said. 'I'm loving it.'

But the RMPs had had enough of watching me and threw me out. It had been a waste of time; they couldn't beast me. They'd told me to do non-stop fitness exercises, and I did.

Another time, during the recruitment, we were on weapons training. We were doing baton training, in case we got sent abroad and had to use the big sticks. For a situation where we needed to arrest someone and they resisted, we were shown how to restrain them by choking them. They chose me to demonstrate the choking technique on. They'd pick on any recruit. As far as they were concerned, you were just a number.

I was down on my knees and the Physical Training Instructor had got the baton across the front of my neck, trying to squeeze and show how little pressure you needed to put on an individual. But I resisted the choking. I flexed my throat muscles. I wouldn't give in, even though my face was turning green and purple.

The PTI said, 'You're going to kill yourself if you keep this up.'

'Yeah,' I croaked. It was willpower. A combination of mental strength and the ability to deny the pain kept me in there. I wasn't going to let a baton beat me.

The instructor gave up. 'Get up,' he said. 'You're mad, you are. Get back in line.' And he picked another recruit for the demonstration. The lad felt the pain and gave in straight away.

Being in the Paras is about proving yourself, or it was then.

You had to get up at five in the morning and, from then on, everything was done on the double. You had your room jobs. This could be cleaning the toilets or whatever you were allotted to do. Then you went into breakfast at six, on the double. Ten minutes for breakfast, then back for kit inspection. But I accepted all this. I adapted to it without a problem. I enjoyed it. It was an ongoing challenge.

But others couldn't take it. They were used to getting a cup of tea in bed at seven. But I was never spoiled as a child, so I didn't feel I was missing out on anything. As a nipper I was just glad to get a breakfast. And the food in the barracks was excellent. Good-quality food. It had to be; an army marches on its stomach. Canteen meals had greatly improved since the National Service days. The army catering corps had chefs who were at least as good as civilian chefs. These guys knew about vitamins and minerals and special diets for physical fitness. They had to. We needed the right fuel, a balanced diet. We were expending energy all the time.

The Paras gave me everything I needed at that time: a mental discipline and physical challenges. Towards the end of the recruitment training, we were sent to Wales for five or six days of exercises in the snow. It was the final selection. If we passed that, we'd be sent straight to RAF Brize Norton, in Oxfordshire, for six weeks of operational parachute training.

I was looking forward to getting there. It was going to be like a holiday camp after the tough regime we'd been through. We were going to be handed over to the RAF, who were a lot more relaxed and laid-back about it all. It would be like being made to do a twenty-six-mile run every day, then suddenly being told, 'It's all right, you only have to do two hundred metres today.' It was going to be a stroll in the park, I reckoned.

By this time we were down to thirty men out of the one hundred who'd begun the training. This situation wouldn't happen now. Standards of selection in certain regiments are much more relaxed. In those days you accepted being pushed around, the bullying. Certain members of staff could dish that out. I remember one soldier with us, he hadn't cleaned his SLR properly. He got the butt of it in his jaw. It put him on his arse. But you saw it and you accepted it. It was part of what it was about. You had to take punishment.

I was beasted by selection staff, but I wouldn't say I was ever bullied. I was never pushed around by people of my own rank. We had a good platoon, a mature group of men, and we were being challenged and tested in other directions. We didn't have time to harass each other. You'd get your kit ready for the next day, then switch off.

When we got to Brize Norton we mixed with other elite squadrons who were there to get their wings. The Royal Marine Commandos were there and the SBS, the Special Boat Service. We were made to jump from different low-level heights with a container. You'd be in the air for about thirty seconds, then land, ready to go into action on the ground. Before joining the Paras I'd been scared of heights, so I'd go with some of the other lads in the evening, in our own time, down to the Paras' assault course.

This was all about heights. You'd be up there, about thirty or forty feet in the air, on a big scaffolding pole. There were one or two of us who had to overcome this fear. You had to get used to the height. If you wanted that red beret, which only a few people can wear, you had to go for it. You'd bust a gut for it.

But I was having a few problems getting it right with the jumps. We practised in a big hangar at ground level and I kept making mistakes. We had to account for wind velocity and I was screwing up big time. If the wind's coming from the north-east, you've got to angle your body to a south-westerly position. Your ankle, knee and hip have to land properly. I wasn't picking up the techniques as fast as some of the others. Well, someone has to be the slowest.

When it came to the actual parachute jumps, I was doing fine, landing properly. We had to do eight jumps and I was coming out of the aircraft perfectly, from between one thousand feet and eight hundred feet. But I didn't realise I was being assessed on the whole training. Every day I was making mistakes and being criticised by the training officers. They don't care what they say to you, and my confidence was at an all-time low. I was getting frustrated with myself. There was an officer there, a lieutenant in the Royal Marine Commandos. Whenever I made a mistake in parachute training, he'd make a remark about me. 'You Irish are thick,' he'd say. And, 'You Paras are thick as anything.'

I'd had enough of this after a couple of weeks. There was a boxing ring at the Brize Norton club. I said to him, 'Let's go down to the boxing club and sort this out.' I went off to the club and found the door locked, so I kicked the door in. The lieutenant followed me down and we put the gloves on. We had it out, there and then.

First round, I took it easy with the guy. Second round, I hit him and cracked his cheekbone and broke his nose. We hadn't needed a referee, but someone came in when the officer was on his back in the second round. The next day I was in the hangar when the lieutenant arrived with a big bandage on. He marched straight up to me.

The selection staff in charge of us were shocked to see what I'd done, that I'd gone ahead after the guy's ragging and hurt him. But I wasn't worried I'd get chucked off the course. I knew I'd settled the matter in the right way, in the boxing ring. The officer had accepted my challenge, but he had to leave the parachute training course because of his injuries.

That day he came up and shook my hand in front of everyone and said, 'Best of luck to you, Doyle.' I think he understood he should have kept his mouth shut earlier. He realised you don't take the piss out of someone. He understood the Paras ain't that bad. He came up to me like a man, as an officer and a gentleman from the Royal Marine Commandos, and shook my hand and apologised.

'Why'd he shake your hand like that, Doyle?' I was asked by the selection staff. I told them how we'd gone down and sorted out our differences in the ring. They replied, 'Fair enough,' and nothing more was said. Come the day of the big parade, the passing-out ceremony where we got our wings, who should get the award for the best parachute student on the course? Private Doyle.

I was sure they'd made a mistake. Someone pushed me forward and I said, 'Have you got this right? I kept making mistakes.'

'You've got this for effort,' they said. 'For trying, and for taking the knocks. For perseverance.' I was chuffed, over the moon. I'd thought everything was going against me: getting it wrong in training sessions in the hangar, then hitting a Royal Marine Commando officer. But I got my parachute wings and I'd got an extra award with it.

A few years later an acquaintance of mine met up with some marines, who said, 'So, you're a friend of Paddy Doyle's? He's the one that gave that Marine Commando a good hiding.'

Well, all I can say is I was provoked. And it was regular provocation. I'd taken about a week of verbal before I finally said, 'Right, I'm not having this.' It's a man's world. I challenged him properly and he failed properly. He was going to be part of the SBS. Presumably he'd passed the water training and needed his parachute wings so he could be dropped into the sea. I probably messed up his selection and he'd have to do the course again some other time. And I'm sure he had some questions to answer when he went before his officers, back at his base. They must have said to him, 'You should never have stepped in that ring.'

It was a big day, after our six months' training, when we passed out at Aldershot. There was a huge parade and we wore our 'number ones', our best kit, as we marched in front of our friends and family. As we stood there in line, they called out the Champion Recruit. It was me. I'd got the Champion Recruit award for the year. But I knew I wasn't the brightest recruit on the course. My senior officer said, 'Doyle, you're the thickest Champion Recruit we've ever had.' Fair enough.

It was my perseverance again. I'd got the award for helping others with, say, fitness courses or kit inspection. I'd go to the back of the course and push lads along if they were falling behind in the running, or I'd help them arrange their boots and uniform for an inspection so they wouldn't make a mistake. It had been noticed I was a team player. But I was a team player for a reason. In the Paras you had to adapt your individuality to function as part of a team.

There was the one thing I didn't like: the constant assessment. They were appraising you day in, day out. It was the first time in my life I'd really had to watch myself and behave well. If I hadn't done, there would have been ten Paras in the room, carting me off to the nick and giving me a good hiding. That was always at the back of my mind. They would have done that.

But there was always sport to compensate. I volunteered to represent the Parachute Regiment in the British Army Cross Country Championships in Aldershot. It was a relay effort. We didn't get anywhere near the teams who won. Our team had been put together too late to be effective, but we did our best. I was glad I'd had my name put forward and been given the challenge, that I'd participated.

The course was about five miles in length, over rough, steep terrain; up hill and down dale where the tanks trained. We not only had to run over deep tracks but up a lot of sand hills that were used for tank exercises. These were a real challenge, as you don't get a grip with your feet on sand: it's two steps forward and four steps back. The hardest thing about cross-country terrain is that you don't know what you're going to come up against next. And for every hill you run down, there's another one to go up. It's a constant effort.

We hadn't had the chance to prepare, plan and train for the event like some of the other teams. We'd done some training but our military exercises were the priority. The Paras were a crack regiment and we had to maintain our standards. We were classed as Special Forces, and weapons training and military exercises were prioritised. We were exercising, but not for sports excellence.

After we passed out we were sent, as fully fledged Paras, to our respective battalions. Towards the end of our training I knew I was being sent to 2 Para, the second battalion of the Parachute Regiment. But something had changed. I was a Para now. The challenge wasn't so great. It was like being a part-timer: getting up at eight o'clock in the morning instead of five. I'd imagined we'd continue with a demanding regime, but it was much more relaxed. I wanted the challenge to continue. I soon got bored with the comparatively easy life. And that's when I reverted to my old behaviour; my pre-army, bar-brawling, confrontational behaviour.

Where were the challenges? It had all stopped. Frustration began to well up in me. Was this what I'd trained for? I applied to go on a few courses, but never got on them. I'd wanted to train as a PTI, but the waiting list for the course was too long. A Heavy Goods Vehicle course: the waiting list was too long. I started going into town and drinking and getting into trouble.

We had time off most weekends and wore civvies to go into town. A couple of months after my passing out, some soldier was giving me grief in a fish and chip shop. He was from another regiment and he was slagging off the Paras. I just turned round and hit him. I've still got the busted hand. I pushed the knuckle back when I hit him and didn't get it set afterwards. I left him on the floor and did a runner with another Para. The civilian police and the military police were all over Aldershot, looking for us. I dodged off into the bushes to avoid the roads and made my way back to the camp. I was never caught for that one.

I wasn't necessarily looking to see action. I was looking for the next phase, the next level in the training. The Pathfinders, the elite regiment, was the next step and that led to the SAS, the Special Air Service. But I wasn't in the army long enough to apply for that. The Paras are the breeding ground for the SAS, but you've got to be in for about five years in order to mature and prove yourself and get all the training under your belt.

I spent about twelve months kicking around Aldershot before life began to change. We knew we were going somewhere. We did our required number of parachute jumps to keep our wings. But I jumped and landed badly, damaging my vertebrae and my shoulder, and ended up in the military hospital at Woolwich. I felt fit after a week but I stayed in for a couple of months. The others had gone on an exercise somewhere, so I thought I'd stay in hospital for a bit longer and enjoy myself. I'd never been so spoilt in all my life. I was really getting to enjoy the hospital food and the nurses.

But after a while I got bored, and one night I sneaked out of the hospital. I headed for a pub near the Royal Artillery Barracks and got drunk. When I came out I was approached by another soldier. I had a Paras sweatshirt on, and to another soldier that's a challenge. Regiments in the British Army are like football teams in their rivalry. He could see from the way I was walking I was far from sober, so he came up to me and said something. And I hit him. Then, out of nowhere, another soldier came at me. And I struck him. Another soldier came along, and I struck him. Word had got out there was a Para zigzagging down the road. Another one came at me. Before I'd gone the three hundred metres back to the hospital, I must have hit about eight Royal Artillery soldiers.

When I saw the helicopters coming over, shining their floodlights everywhere, I knew I had to get back to my hospital bed. The civilian police were everywhere, so I hid in the bushes and waited. I managed to sneak into the hospital and made it into the reception area. Then the receptionist started shouting at me, 'Where've you been?'

I was still drunk. I grabbed him by the lapels and pulled him over the reception desk. As I pulled him towards me, somebody else grabbed me by the legs. Then the military police came charging in and batoned me. They gave me a good hiding and hauled me off to the Royal Artillery prison cells.

Still drunk and fighting anyone who came near me, I was locked up in a cell. I went berserk and wrecked the place, as far as

I could, urinating over the floor and punching the walls. They left me there for the night to sober up. I thought, Sod it. I was twenty-two, selfish and I didn't give a damn about anyone else. I was still aggressive and a brawler, in spite of my army training. Well, a leopard doesn't change its spots, does it?

About nine o'clock the next morning a guard of about ten officers appeared in my cell. They were taking no chances: on went the handcuffs. I was bundled into the back of a Land Rover and driven back to the hospital, where the officers had a word with the doctors. Their opinion was that there was nothing wrong with me, that I was having a field day to get out of doing exercises back at Aldershot. Which I was.

More boring army exercises. I'd done enough of them. But they sent me back to Aldershot, on my own, on the train. Odd that. But when I got back, I was hauled up in front of my commanding officer. I got another month in jail. They told me I could have got six months.

Life's hard in an army nick. Your head is shaved down to nothing, so it's obvious to everyone you're a prisoner. They take the laces out of your boots, so you can't do a runner. Your pay is stopped. They give you extra fitness exercises. You do all the dirty jobs around the camp, sweeping and cleaning up all the muck. There's inspection at six o'clock every morning. Your cell has to be set out in a certain way. No dust, boots polished. I just accepted it. I knew what I'd done wrong and went along with the consequences. I couldn't complain.

In fact, I was happier with a tougher regime. I'd been bored before. I fitted into the prison routine well. I even enjoyed it. The best thing was the extra PT every day. It was supposed to be beasting, but I loved it all. One day I was in real trouble. I'd left a bit of dust in my cell. A regimental police officer called me out to beast me.

I was given a sixty-pound Second World War wombat shell and told to do step-ups with it. Stepping up and down with this sixty-pound bombshell, they expected me to last five minutes. They could see me sweating. And I'm still at it after half an hour.

'Are you finished, Doyle?'

'No, staff. Not finished.' Up and down, up and down; I'm still in there. I'm back to the kind of exercise I'd enjoyed as a recruit. Instead of press-ups, it was a wombat shell. I could still do it now.

After four weeks of that, I was out. The army must have realised I needed a challenge to keep me interested, and they put me down for Patrols Company, an elite unit within the Paras. You had to go on a separate selection course for this 'C' Company in 2 Para. At first I was half-hearted about joining. I had to go to Wales again to do the log-carrying exercises, the endurance training and the assault courses I'd done before.

The logs were the size of telephone poles and weighed about one hundred pounds. Eight of us had to carry one along a five-mile course. The assault courses involved going through tunnels of water, scaling heights and sheer faces, and rope work. There were navigational exercises where we were set up to be attacked by a so-called enemy and we had to 'bug out', or get out of the situation, with all our kit intact. Senior staff officers were the enemy and they 'attacked' at three o'clock in the morning. After we'd got out fast, plus kit, we had to go straight into a ten-mile march. If you left anything behind, it was a strike against you. That's what selection is about. Our backpacks weighed about sixty or seventy pounds.

Well, I didn't mind doing it, and I passed. I was sent out to Oman for six weeks with a hundred and fifty other Paras. There were sniper units with us and we did six weeks of live firing exercises. We jumped in the desert, practising our parachute skills in a new terrain, ready for any situation we might be dropped into. It's important for troops in armies all over the world to be able to adapt to foreign terrains and conditions.

Those weeks were hard and hot, but I enjoyed it. At the end of the six weeks we were given a couple of days off. But Oman is a Muslim country: they don't drink alcohol. This is bad news for a hundred and fifty paratroopers. The government wouldn't allow us let our hair down in Muscat, the capital. They probably knew we'd wreck it. So they took us off the mainland and put us on an island, surrounded by shark-infested water. They gave us each a crate of Heineken and for two days we relaxed and got drunk and raised our beer cans to the sharks.

To kill time during our R&R, our rest and recuperation, I'd taken along a couple of pairs of boxing gloves. Any of the lads on the island who wanted to box could get together with me and have a go. We just knocked hell out of each other to kill time. It was like prize fighting. I busted one guy's nose and gave another quite a few headaches. I was very fit at the time. I was exercising daily and training in good weather and we were eating salads every day, so I was coming out on top. By this time I would never lose a fight. It just didn't happen.

But my natural inclination for confrontation wasn't always good news. During my time in Oman, I had a sergeant major who was always finding fault with what I did. He was nearing retirement and I think he was winding me up to get a reaction. Friction developed between us and this went on for a while. My temper was being pushed to the limit.

One day I was put in charge of the GPMG on a desert exercise. But the weapon got blocked with sand and it wouldn't fire. I was pretty frustrated about that myself, and I didn't need someone else to start on at me. An officer bawled me out and, in the heat of the day, my patience snapped. I could only see red. I swung the gun round and pointed it at him, forgetting it was still full of live ammunition.

'You do bloody better then!' I yelled at him.

At that point I was arrested. I was escorted back to camp in a Range Rover and confined to my tent.

I waited in that hot, stuffy tent, feeling angry and frustrated. Then the sergeant major who'd made a point of criticising me all the time came into the tent. He started shouting at me some more, I don't know what for. He seemed to be enjoying the situation I was in. But I'd reached boiling point. I lost my rag with the guy. I threw my boots at him, then my bergen, my military rucksack. I chucked everything in the tent at him. Then I chased him outside.

I don't think that had ever been done before. And the bastard ran hell for leather.

If I ever see that guy again, I'd probably rag-doll him. I reckon he stabbed me in the back by putting in a report about my behaviour, and that was to have serious repercussions when I got back to England. What did the army want of me? I'd been trained to be aggressive, fit and ready to fight. But my energy and my potential had been mishandled and misdirected, as far as I was concerned. I was a good soldier and I wanted to get on in the regiment, make progress. I don't believe the army always convert the talent they have.

I was the right material for them. Where was the encouragement to develop that? I'd joined the Parachute Regiment. I'd spent six months doing one of the hardest recruitment courses in the world. Then it was off to the battalion, where discipline was suddenly relaxed. You'd get up at eight, you'd have an hour's lunch, twelve till one, and you'd finish at four every day. It was more like a part-time job than a demanding professional career. It was only when we went on exercises that the pace changed. I needed to be stretched. If I wasn't, boredom would set in and I'd rebel.

During the more casual periods I was out running, down the gym or in the army boxing centre or the PT centre. I had to find my own outlets for my energy, my own challenges. I had to keep my interest up. My face fitted, but not my temperament. And I wasn't the only one who had this problem. There were quite a few others who felt as I did, who were looking to be stretched.

* * *

Meanwhile I was having a good time. I was travelling a bit and I was quite happy with what I was doing and where I was. But when I came back from Oman, it was time to do other things. Because of the scrapes I'd been in over the last two years, my behavioural problems, as the army saw it, I wasn't able to sign up again. I'd been a bad lad and I'd lost that option.

Army contracts are renewed every three years. When I'd gone out to Oman, I still had the Woolwich incident, where I'd laid into the eight soldiers, hanging over me. I'd done my spell in the clink but I still had to go before a disciplinary hearing committee. The room was full of officers. They said I'd caused the trouble, I'd started the fights. I insisted I'd been defending myself. The problem was being a Para, having a red beret. I reckon Paras are stigmatised; they're considered troublemakers. I had eight officers, who weren't in the Paras, maintaining it was my fault. I was up against it. So, what chance?

Added to that was the incident where I'd pointed a machine gun with live rounds in it at an officer. Plus, I'd chased a sergeant major through the camp. My problem is, if someone challenges me verbally, I challenge them verbally too. I always react. I was a good soldier: I could jump out of a plane and shoot and kill, but I'd always react. I was never one to let myself be bullied. As far as chasing the sergeant major was concerned, I felt I'd been wound up, provoked, and I pounced. They hadn't been able to put me in jail for that in the middle of the desert, so they let me carry on with the exercise and the training until I got back.

It took some time to gather together all my fighting

misdemeanours for the hearing. Military hearings are not like civilian affairs. I think the agenda had been set and the decision made before I went into the room. I think the army realised they'd got a headbanger, partly of their own making. Basically I was told that my behaviour couldn't be tolerated and they listed my different confrontations. I pointed out that I was trained to be fit, aggressive and to react. I'd made some mistakes and all of a sudden they couldn't handle it. But that didn't win the day. I wanted to continue in the Paras, but I wasn't invited to reapply. I accepted it. It was time to move on.

CHAPTER 6

GOING THE EXTRA MILE

WHEN I CAME OUT of the Paras, I didn't go back to supermarket work. First thing I did was head for London. I'd seen a job advertised in an Aldershot paper and I ended up with a management position in a security firm. I wasn't doing the day-to-day work; I was overseeing up to two hundred blokes who were on the night shift. The business covered an area from the Elephant and Castle in the south, right across central London to the north, providing security for the best hotels and other organisations. The firm's offices were in Vauxhall Bridge Road and I found myself a flat further south, in Streatham, at the back end of Brixton.

My job was to oversee the security guards: checking they were on site on time and dressed properly, disciplining them and promoting them as necessary. I managed and co-ordinated my area during the night, dealing with emergencies a lot of the time.

Sometimes a security guard on a certain site would have a problem and he'd call me in to sort it out. In the last resort, if I couldn't deal with it, I'd call in the emergency services. The job carried a lot of responsibility. I had to get around as many sites as possible and check that everything was working smoothly. I'd have a cup of coffee with the guard and make sure he was OK, then move on to the next site.

Having just come out of the army, I was in the right frame of mind to oversee schedules and uniforms. I'd originally gone for a job as a security guard with the firm, but when they talked to me they wanted me as an inspector. For a while I drove around, keeping an eye on the guards on site, then I was promoted to Senior Inspector, which meant I was in charge of the control room staff monitoring the screens and manning the phones back at headquarters. The money wasn't so bad and my flat was only about £20 a week. I was renting a room in a house owned by a couple of immigrant brothers. They were also security guards in the firm. Lovely lads; I'll never forget them. Our arrangement was basically that they rented out the room cheaply to me and, in return, I'd recommend them for a small pay rise.

This particular security business supplied guards for the Canary Wharf development in Docklands and I had to supervise the night shift. One night I was called out by a security guard, a Nigerian who was over here doing a college course. He was stuck in a hut on this big, barren site. He said, 'Paddy, we've got three or four tramps down here, drunk. They won't move off site. They're making a big fire.'

I got in the van and drove down to the fire, with the security guard bringing up the rear. It was my job to make sure my staff were all right. 'I'll sort it out,' I said. And I went over and asked the tramps to leave. But the situation started to get confrontational: verbally, not violently. The tramps had bottles and I could see the knives they were using to eat their meal around the fire. One of them got up and came over to me. We faced each other, nose to nose. He stank. His breath was like a blowtorch in my face. I said to him, 'If you don't leave, mate, I'm going to make you leave.'

I crossed to the fire and put it out in front of them. We waited. After about fifteen or twenty minutes the tramps got up and started to leave the site, shouting abuse as they went. The security guard turned to me and smiled and shook his head. 'You got a lot o' balls, man!' he laughed.

Another time my fitness training came in handy was in a fish and chip shop near the Territorial Army centre in Chelsea. I'd stopped to get something to eat halfway through my night shift; I was starving. Standing there, waiting for my food, I noticed a big guy looking at me. He was tall: six foot four or five. He was dressed fairly smartly. Shaven head.

My security company shirt might have intrigued him. It had epaulettes on the shoulders. I might have looked like some sort of policeman. I collected my fish and chips and went outside to my van. I noticed the man was walking behind me. What worried me was he didn't have any fish and chips in his hands. No pie, no kebab, nothing. I had to think fast. I kept going. Having been in the army, I was trained to look for certain signs of behaviour in people. I was switched on to potential situations. He was still there, following me.

I turned off down an alley, as if to go to the toilet. The big guy was right behind me, looking at me, getting closer. Then he came up beside me. I knew something was going to go off. I was in two minds: he either fancied me or he wanted a fight. I knew I could look after myself. In those days it was either do or die. I didn't hesitate.

I threw the first punch. I hit him on the jaw, not realising the bloke would go flying up in the air. It was like something out of a Hollywood movie: he landed on a load of boxes. I went over and checked him out. The alley was well lit, and I could see he was snoring. I headed back to the van, about four or five hundred metres away, and drove off as fast as I could. I never got to eat my fish and chips. Next night I went back and found the spot where I'd hit the geezer. Nothing there to see except dried blood all around.

I've got to make it clear at this point; that it's not aggression that gets me into, and out of, these kinds of situations. It's the work I do. Where I go, there's trouble. It's my job to confront it, not run away from it. It's a question of survival. Maybe it's the way I look, my natural wariness of others. Somehow trouble always seems to beat a path to my door. And I have to deal with it.

And the type of sport I've been involved in over the years has tended to give me a certain reputation. I'm judged before I've done anything. I'm not one to look for trouble, never have been. I don't like confrontations. They're a pain in the arse. Blood and gore don't turn me on. I'd rather study at college or have a quiet meal with my girl. I like to socialise and hold reasonable conversations. But, sometimes, things have happened in a certain way. It's been the nature of the jobs I've had.

Some books will idolise a character for being nasty and aggressive. I've experienced my share of violence, but not because I've gone looking for it. It was the name of the game. It's what I had to do. People employed me for that and expected me to survive in threatening situations. Maybe some of it had to do with body language, the way I stand. I glance at someone; they look at me and think, He looks tough. I'm thinking, What's he staring at? I was trained to look out for that, right from my early days as a boy, learning judo. You learn to counter-punch, to meet a challenge, automatically.

One day I had a bit of a run-in with the manager of the security firm. The guy was ex-forces but I reckoned his style of management wasn't right. We had a verbal confrontation in front of the office staff, and I told him where to get off. In my opinion he wasn't doing the job properly. He wasn't giving people the support and back-up. But that was it for me; I wanted to leave quietly. I'd had enough of London and working nights and sorting out other people's problems. I left a couple of days later, and didn't even give notice I was leaving. I went straight back to the flat, picked up my kit and came back to Birmingham.

I hadn't really practised any serious sport while I was in

London. I'd run on my own in the streets around Streatham and I went to a boxing club a couple of times, just to do some training: punchbag work, shadow boxing and skills training. Skills training involves skipping, pad work and circuit training: all the techniques you have to hone for the ring. The club I went to produced some top amateur boxers, I remember.

I settled in at my mum's when I got back to Birmingham. I had no idea what I wanted to do. I started with a couple of agency jobs, doing temporary warehouse work. This helped me find my feet, got me back into the swing of things. At that time I didn't feel like taking on jobs with a lot of responsibility. I only enjoy management jobs when it's something I really want to do, something I'm really interested in. That's why I haven't gone into running a chain of gyms. I like to be 'hands on', not tied to a desk. I don't mind managing a business where I'm in the field and on the move. I've always been a traveller. A job in the field brings variety and keeps my mind stimulated. I don't feel I'm stagnating. I feel the opposite: alive. Best of all, I like to have a lot of different strings to my bow, businesswise.

I got some part-time work at the NEC, the National Exhibition Centre, in Birmingham. There were always stands to put up and take down for the different exhibitions. This type of work, along with the warehouse temping, lasted about four or five months. It gave me a chance to get back into sports and I started weight training at the Harborne club again.

As far as I know, I'm the only one in the group of friends I had as a lad who later channelled his energy into sport, certainly to the level I got to. That was down to self-discipline, but the army put the finishing touches to that by giving me more discipline. And when I left, I decided to push my capabilities further. The army knocked the chip off my shoulder. I already had the interest in sport, and the energy. What the army gave me was discipline. And that's why I joined the Paras. The Paras are known for their hard outlook, their aggressive way of dealing with a situation and their level of fitness. Their standards of professionalism sorted me out. Otherwise it would have been prison.

By this time I was beginning to settle down again and find a routine. I looked around for a permanent position and got a job as a clerk with Birmingham City Council's Housing Department. Soon I was made a Scale 2 clerk, then a Scale 3 clerk, and from there I applied for the post of Housing Estates Officer. This suited my temperament and personality much more. It got me away from the desk work. I was out and about on the estates, dealing with the neighbourhood watch, housing associations and emergency services. I was always here and there, dealing with rent arrears and other problems. I really loved that job.

I'd not long been promoted to Housing Estates Officer, based at the Ladywood Labour Office, when we had a problem with a tenant. The man was psychologically disturbed and had been chasing children who lived in the same block. A parent had phoned the office and said his daughter was being frightened by this man. The guy had been running up and down the hallways, sometimes with a knife in his hand. We checked him out and found he'd been in All Saints, a local mental hospital, and had been treated for violent behaviour.

The other housing officers in my office took one look at the background information to this particular problem and passed the form on to the next desk. No one wanted to deal with this nutter. I'd worked in other council estates in Birmingham, such as New Town and Nechells, where the crime rate was high, but here I was, new on the patch, green around the gills, and not knowing which problems I should be avoiding.

'Paddy, can you deal with this?' someone said to me one morning.

I took the file. 'Yeah, I'll look after it. I'll deal with this one.'

Then they told me what the problem was: how this guy had a history of violent behaviour when he'd been approached by the police and other authorities.

But I'd accepted the case. So round there I went. I found the caretaker sweeping in front of the flats.

'What floor is this bloke on?' I showed him the name and address on the file I had with me.

The caretaker stopped sweeping, leant on his broom and looked at me. 'Don't think I'm going up there with you,' he said.

'I'd like you to come along, as a witness, if there's any trouble,' I explained.

'No fuckin' way. I'm not going with you. You're on your own. I know what the guy's like.'

I shrugged. 'Suit yourself.' I made my way up the stairs, went along the hallway, found the door and knocked. I was still knocking when it opened. Big guy, three or four inches taller than me. He looked as though he was going to hit me. I knew his history. My instinct was to hit him first, straight away and seriously. And I did just that.

The guy had a jaw like granite. He fell back against the wall but his eyes were still fixed on me, like two laser beams. I reckoned he was going back into his kitchen to grab a knife, so I said immediately, 'Follow me.' And I marched him outside and down to the end of the corridor. 'Look,' I said, jabbing my finger at him, 'this is my fuckin' patch now. I'm the Housing Estates Officer for Ladywood and I don't want any more problems from you.'

The guy stared at me with a wild look. 'Who are you?' he demanded. And, as he said this, I happened to look up. I could see his fist marks in the plaster of the ceiling above us.

Quickly, I carried on lecturing him, as though he were a kid. I was about twenty-four or twenty-five at the time, and he was probably a few years older than me, about thirty, I reckon. But he seemed to have the mentality of a teenager or a child. I said to him, 'Stop chasing children down the corridor. No more messing about.'

His eyes bored into me.

'OK, that's it for now,' I said. 'I'll be back later.' I had no intention of coming back for another round with this lunatic. I started to walk away from him. And he started running in the opposite direction, back to the flat. All I could think of was the knife he had back there. I ran like hell down to the ground floor. I wanted to put as much space as possible between him and me.

Later we had to get the guy committed. He caused some more trouble in the flats and he didn't leave us much choice. The police weren't allowed to touch him because of his mental instability, so we phoned his social worker. Next thing, some people came round to inject him and take him away.

Then he was released back into society. What he was doing wasn't looked on as a crime, probably because he wasn't responsible for his actions. About a month later he set fire to his flat. This time it was a matter for the police. And which sergeant should go round to arrest him? My friend, Wayne, who trained with me in the evenings, from Ladywood Police Station.

Wayne said to him, 'Someone gave you a hiding the other week, didn't they?'

The nutter says, 'How d'you know? How d'you know that?'

And Wayne says, 'I know, mate. I know.'

Another time while I was working on the Housing Team, a tenant came into the office. This guy was drunk and abusive and started threatening the staff. They asked me to interview him. Me again. During the interview the bloke tried to hit me and headbutt me. Naturally I restrained him and frogmarched him off the premises.

But the guy was still feeling aggrieved about a letter he'd received for rent arrears. He produced a Stanley knife and threatened me again. I took the knife off him, then stood and watched while he walked away, shouting and swearing.

While I was with the Housing Department I felt a lot of problems were being passed on to me to sort out. But I didn't have the personality to put up with these situations. I had a feeling that one day there'd be an incident where I'd get into trouble sorting out other people's problems. With my sports career coming along and the way things were going at work, I knew it was time for me to leave.

During my time with Birmingham City Council, I'd got back into my weight training and I continued to run on my own. Then, one weekend in 1987, during my first year as a housing clerk, I went to a flea market in Warwick with my girlfriend at that time. We stopped at a second-hand stall and I picked up a dog-eared copy of *The Guinness Book of World Records*. I was flicking through the pages and came across the press-ups section. I looked at the records and thought, Well, I can do better than that. I bought the book and back at home I took a good look at the records.

I was already training pretty hard, so I thought I'd put my fitness to good use. But I wanted to do something different. I'd seen a particular record in the annual *Strength and Speed Record Book* edited by Dale Harder. This is an excellent publication that covers strength and endurance and speed events. I started to focus my training. I wanted to go for the press-ups world record with a fifty-pound steel plate on my back. The record had been set about fifteen years previously and I wanted to break it. Another book I used to read was *The Alternative Book of Records*. In fact, there were a number of record books I used to come across when I was training in various gyms, but *The Guinness Book of World Records* is the most distinguished.

To attempt to break a world record takes time and organisation.

I had to work out how many hours a day I needed to train and who would be training with me. I had a good friend called Desi Clifton. We'd met in a club in Birmingham about five years earlier. I'd known him before I'd gone into the army and he'd come to my passing-out parade. I spoke to Desi about going for a record and he said he'd like to come on board and help out with the training and preparation.

Desi is a former karate instructor. He's a few years older than me and was able to give me a lot of tips. He helped me a great deal with my training, using the stopwatch. We gelled as a team. He supported me solidly and became a loyal coach. He was with me on nearly every record attempt for the first five or six years. If I was going for a backpack record, running in an endurance event or a marathon, Desi would be there by the side of me, on his bike. If I was doing press-ups, he'd be there counting them. If I was boxing, he'd be there with the pads for me. He was with me right up to the very last record attempt.

Then other lads from the gym, and different gyms nearby, offered to help put me through my paces. The nucleus of a team was beginning to form: people who would help with my schedule and assist me in keeping fit. Another good friend, who was with me for four or five years, was John McBean, a former Amateur Boxing Association champion who went on to fight professionally at cruiserweight level. He was a great help with my training as well as on the keep-fit side. He really pushed me on. He came out running with me and trained with me in the gym. As a former professional boxer, he was able to give me a lot of advice with pad work. It was only when he became a family man, in the mid-nineties, that he had to restrict the help he could give me. But he got the best out of me in those early days, from about 1990.

John's knowledge and motivation helped me tremendously. He was very loyal and supportive and professional, just like Desi. You need a loyal team around you. It's all about teamwork. Without Desi and guys like John and, later, Paul Jones, I don't think I could have achieved what I have today. Sometimes, when I felt a bit down during training, they were there and picked me up again.

My family were also very supportive, right from the beginning. My sister, my brother and my mother were all as pleased as Punch with what I was doing. When they saw my name in the paper, having a go and doing well, it was great for our morale as a family. My sadness was that my father, who'd died in 1985, when I was in the army, wasn't around to see what I was doing. He'd always been proud of the sports that I'd done in the past.

I broke my first record in May 1987, while I was still working for Birmingham City Council. I did four thousand, one hundred press-ups with a fifty-pound plate on my back, a record category that's developed from ordinary press-ups records. Two weightlifting plates were taped together and put on my back. By lifting from the shoulders, I avoided damaging my spine. Desi and Ralph Farqharson, my friend who ran the Harborne gym, were able to give me the techniques for this. It was in those early days that I got lucky. A valuable team assembled themselves around me.

To set up a record-breaking event, you have to lay out every detail of the attempt in a letter to *The Guinness Book of World Records*. It tells you in the book what you need to do and where to apply. They have to know what record you're going for and when. This gives them the chance to let you know if someone else is attempting the record the day before. If you go for a set number of press-ups, it might have been surpassed the previous day, so you'd be wasting your time and effort. It's hard enough to do a record attempt without wondering if someone else, a few hours earlier, in Hong Kong or Russia, has already beaten it.

It's a big learning curve the first time you get all the paperwork together for the book's editorial team. They respond by sending you their rules and guidelines, which you have to follow for the event. One of the requirements is that you have to approach a governing body or association and ask them to supply officials to monitor the attempt. The officials draw up the documentation by which the record attempt is judged: the rules and regulations that will apply on the day.

To claim a record, you need signed documents which confirm the conditions under which the event took place. You need witnesses' signatures, photos and video footage of the attempt, plus your own signed statement to the event. It's a lot to put in place. It's hard. Sometimes it's harder than doing the actual event. Every detail has to be accounted for before you can claim a record. You don't achieve these titles by sending in a letter telling the editorial team what you've done. It takes a good two weeks after an event to assemble all the information they need. But we never had any problems or queries. We were always thorough in submitting the paperwork and they were always very thorough in checking it.

They don't send along one of their own officials to an event, simply because there are just too many records being challenged all the time. Instead they ask you to use officials in the governing body of the particular sport your record attempt comes under. My first world-record attempt took place on 28 May 1987 at Calthorpe Old Boys' Club, in the centre of Birmingham.

There had been various records set by athletes with weights on their backs, or rather their shoulders. For this first event I went for a time record wearing the fifty-pound plate. There was no set number of press-ups to go for at that time, so I went for four thousand plus the weight on my shoulders, although on the day I managed four thousand, one hundred. The previous record had been forty press-ups wearing a seventy-five-pound weight. I think a guy in the USA had done three hundred press-ups with a three-hundred-pound man holding a thirty-five-pound plate on his back. Another man did one hundred and forty press-ups with three people on his back. So there were different records within the category in the *Strength and Speed Record Book*.

At my first record attempt the British Amateur Weight Lifting Association officiated, in conjunction with the West Midlands Police. At the time I was focused on that one event. I had my sights on the venue and doing the press-ups and breaking that one record; I wasn't looking beyond that. I had no idea I'd go on and break more. It just took off after that first world record. I loved the buzz I got from the challenge.

The preparation for the attempt took three months of training.

It was about the right amount of time I needed. If you're fit anyway, all you have to do is work on your strength and stamina. My back-up team, people like Desi and John, would say to me, 'OK, you've got to work harder on this or that.' Right from the start we devised a training programme for each of my records. We broke it down into what was needed for each event. This can involve running, boxing, circuit training and martial-arts workouts in punching and kicking. The circuit training ensured that my whole body was toned up: the calves, the quads, the arms. The body is transformed into a solid mass of muscle. Then you focus on the fine tuning.

My training for that first event took about two hours a day. It mostly consisted of press-ups wearing the forty-pound weight. But it involved running, as well, with Desi on his bicycle. It had to be in the evenings because I was working during the day. I soon learnt to be very disciplined. Some evenings I'd be tired after a day's work. But I'd get my act together and go down to the gym and do the training. At the Harborne gym I'd do press-ups with other weightlifters standing on my back, to develop the power in my shoulders and my body. These guys would weigh between fourteen and sixteen stone. After doing thirty or forty press-ups with them on top of me, I'd go back to ordinary press-ups.

I used to go out in the evenings to different pubs in the centre of Birmingham. When people heard I was preparing for a world-record attempt with a weight on my back, I used to get challenged. People would lay bets on how many press-ups I could do with someone standing on my back. So I ended up making money through bets at different clubs and pubs. I'd just be standing there, having a shandy, and some guy would bet me I couldn't do a hundred press-ups with so-and-so standing on my back. Often, a group of lads would bet among themselves, then they'd approach me collectively with a bet. So I'd do the press-ups with someone on my shoulders who was using the bar to balance himself. It didn't bother me at all. I'd take on any challenge, any time. It paid for my next round of drinks and a taxi home.

Soon I found I was looking forward to the event. I was starting to get excited about it, as well as making a bit of money on the side. Until the morning of the record attempt. Then I was very nervous. But that's only natural.

The attempt was scheduled for twelve noon. I got up about half-seven and went for a walk to stretch off. I turned up at the venue an hour before we were due to start. I got changed, met the officials and looked at where I'd be doing the attempt. During the countdown to the start, I had to contend with a chronic bout of nervousness. This took the form of nervous energy. I was wound up, coiled like a spring, ready for action, but, at the same time, worried that something might go wrong. The record event would take over four hours of hard work. It's not like going for the hundred metres. Anything could happen, in the first minute or the fifty-ninth minute.

Endurance events, as the name implies, last a long time. If you pull a hamstring in a hundred-metres event, you can finish the race if you've got some grit and determination. But if you get a strained back at the beginning of a four-hour record attempt and your body's being constantly pounded in the same place all the time, you need a different approach and type of fitness, a different kind of concentration and mental toughness, and threshold of pain. You have to be able to persevere, to carry on.

That first record attempt went on for four and a half hours. I had an idea how long a certain number of press-ups would take, but a new category of record was being set, so it was down to me. On the day I just wanted to get the attempt out of the way as fast as I could. I did as many press-ups as I could before I dropped, and that was it. Desi was there, keeping an eye on me, and my friend Wayne Bernstein from the West Midlands Police, plus some other officials I hadn't met before.

It was the first of the record attempts Desi would go through with me. And he did go through it with me. He felt the buzz. He felt the nervous tension. It was contagious. It was passed around. Anyone who was in close proximity just before an event tended to get the vibes. If I was in a bad mood, everyone else suffered. Desi, loyal as ever, was watching me carefully: timing me, motivating me, supporting me. When I started to get tired, he'd spur me on, telling me how many press-ups I had left to do, telling me to pace myself and get my breathing right.

The press-ups were done in sets of ten to twenty, with about thirty seconds' break between each set. You need breaks in order to have a drink of water or relieve yourself. Desi was checking me out for injuries but there were also medics there, like St John's Ambulance. You're required to have a medical support unit for a record attempt. If I'd done something to injure myself, the officials would have stopped the event. It was their job to stop me if I didn't know when to stop, if I was damaging myself, either physically or mentally. During a record-breaking event your mental state is tested as much as your physical state.

After a record attempt like that, you're totally drained, not just physically but also psychologically. The amount of mental energy you use in concentration, in willing yourself to go beyond the pain threshold, is almost unimaginable. The mind suffers as much as the body. After the event you're totally spaced out. You're just not with it, for anybody. You're out of it. Physically and mentally exhausted.

I had an idea it was going to be like that. I'd been doing sets of press-ups in the gym, training for the attempt. But, on the day, when you have the crowd atmosphere and the officials and the cameras, it's a completely different thing. A public event is draining. Training in the gym is the easy part. But whether you can cut it in front of a crowd and a set of officials, that's another matter. Then it's for real. You're on the spot. One chance at it.

It was a comparatively small venue that first time, with about a hundred people there. But that was a good show for a first record attempt. The local press and other media spread the word and that helped me get psyched up for the day. I wanted to go for it. Get it under my belt. That first record still stands today.

On the day it's easy to get agitated, verbally punchy. But you have your team around you. They keep the whole thing calm and concentrated on the event. As well as the general public and the local press, I had my family and friends there. Four thousand, one hundred press-ups were enough for me. I was tired then. But I'd done it. And I was presented with a massive trophy, one of the largest on my shelves at home. My good friend Ralph Farqharson, as Secretary of the British Amateur Weight Lifting Association, presented the award to me. He's a well-respected figure in the weightlifting world.

Afterwards I was interviewed by the *Birmingham Evening Mail* and WM, the West Midlands radio station, as well as BBC TV's *Pebble Mill*. The *Birmingham Evening Mail* gave me an excellent write-up. I was also trying to raise money for a young lad called Christopher Forrest, who was seriously ill at the time. We raised over £1,000 for him, I believe. You always remember your first record attempt. It was the first foot on the ladder to success in a minority sports category. I'd been bitten by the bug. I immediately started thinking about which record to go for next.

Between the ages of twenty-three and twenty-seven I earned money doing door work and sorting out problems for businessmen. Shady deals, but nothing to do with drugs. The business was mostly connected with the porno game. It was porno shop against porno shop, and that's a very ruthless circle. I knew some of the people who were involved in this. They'd say to me, 'Paddy, can you go along and have a word with such-and-such a person?' It would always be at their home address.

The messages I delivered were never physical ones. Only verbal. But one time I turned up somewhere with a balaclava on my head. I had two black guys with me from the gym. They're good lads, good friends. And I had a brown paper bag over my hand; it looked as though I was carrying a shotgun. I felt justified: the guy had been selling child pornography. I stood there and pointed my hand and said, 'You know what you've done. Don't do it again.' I got paid well for that, I remember. The night work wasn't regular and I'd be doing odd jobs in the daytime. I'd be down the gym and hanging about. Then I got arrested.

I was twenty-three and I'd not long been back in training at the Harborne Weight Training Centre for my first world-record attempt. While I was at the club there was an ex-RAF physical training instructor working out there. Then a group of us in the gym, including him, decided to go down to Wales for a weekend and do some walking. The ex-PTI knew the terrain we were heading for, so I asked him what he thought we should wear. He said to me, 'Just wear your trainers, Paddy.' So I did.

Cut to Wales. Well, being me, I got ahead of everybody else on a mountain walk in Snowdonia. I went up the mountain and the mist came down. I was about a hundred metres in front of the group and I took a path I thought the others would be going along. After about twenty metres I found I had to start climbing down some rocks, but I reckoned the others would be catching me up soon. It was only after a hundred metres or so that I realised I'd taken the wrong path. And what I could see, about twenty metres away, was two guys going up past me, using ropes and wearing helmets. They looked at me and said, 'What are you doing?'

And I said, 'What are you doing?'

'Where are your ropes and boots?' they asked. 'You're climbing down a rock face.'

There I was, in my cheap trainers with my cheap and skimpy rucksack. Suddenly I started to slip. I lost my grip on the rocks. Then I fell.

I landed about four or five metres below, in a crevice at the mouth of a cave. My ankle was twisted and badly bruised and I couldn't get out of the space I'd fallen into. I shouted and the climbers heard me. They made their way over to me, saw the problem and phoned the RAF air-rescue service. Next thing, I was being winched up in the air. The RAF guys said to me, 'We thought you had a broken leg with a fall like that.'

'No,' I told them. 'I've only twisted my ankle.' I knew I'd been lucky there. But I was checked out and X-rayed at the hospital. And, sure enough, it was a twisted ankle. They bandaged it up, gave me some crutches and sent me on my way.

Meanwhile the ex-PT instructor and the others had waited near the top of the mountain for me. When they couldn't find me, they thought I'd gone ahead. They'd spent another two or three hours walking, expecting to find me, not realising I'd taken the wrong path and had an accident. Eventually they'd phoned the police and found out where I was and arrived at the hospital. When I saw the guy who'd advised me to wear cheap trainers for that walk, I saw red and purple and all the colours. I reckoned he could have got me killed. I was convinced the supervision of the group was down to him. He should have said, 'Don't go down this path, take this one.' But his attitude to the situation was different. He reckoned it was my own fault. And he let me know he wasn't that bothered about what had happened to me.

Next thing I knew, I was chasing this bloke down the road on my crutches. I was yelling at him, 'I'll kill you!' and waving my sticks. But I couldn't catch him. So I threw my crutches at him and hopped after him on one leg. But he made sure I didn't get to him, or anywhere close.

A few years later during a training session with the Harborne gym, when I was out running with a pal, who should I bump into, but the guy I'd blamed for getting me lost on the mountain top in Wales. He'd gone on to join the police force and I'd heard he'd been telling people he wasn't afraid of me coming after him. So we had the confrontation, there and then. I punched him on the nose and watched the blood run. Honour was satisfied as far as I was concerned, and I went back to the gym.

And that's where I was, training with my friends Wayne Bernstein, who's now a Detective Inspector, and Tyrone Powell, who's now a Detective Constable, both with West Midlands Police. Wayne was a sergeant at the time, based at Smethwick, and both men were good pals, helping me out by officiating at my world-record attempts during those first couple of years. I heard the familiar sound getting louder. Louder. Police sirens.

Three panda cars pulled up outside the building. In came a police officer. He went up to Ralph and said, 'Is Paddy Doyle here?'

'He's down there,' said Ralph, pointing to where I was training.

And the strange thing was, with all those police cars outside, only one young constable had come into the building. He looked as though it was his first day on the job. There must have been about six or seven officers out there. They probably thought that if they'd all marched into the gym, it would have looked intimidating and caused friction. But the young officer handled himself well. He came over to me and asked, 'Paddy Doyle?'

'Yes?'

'I'm going to arrest you for assaulting a serving police officer.'

Immediately one of the guys with me said, 'Paddy, don't say anything. Go to the station with the officer.' So they took me away to the Ladywood station. Funnily enough, this is next door to Tesco at Edgbaston, where I'd been warned by the police officer in the car park all those years before. The districts of Ladywood and Edgbaston are next door to each other.

Inside the station, they took me through the procedure. After taking away my personal possessions, they put me in a cell. I sat there and did some thinking. And I thought I'd better come up with something pretty quick. I knew if I got convicted of assaulting a police officer, I'd be doing time. I was in serious trouble. So I punched myself in the eye.

Sitting in the interview room with my black eye, my story would have been, 'Well, look what the guy did to me.' One of my pals I'd been running with had given me that tip. 'If you get arrested, tell them he hit you as well,' he said.

'OK,' I'd said. But it hurts when you punch yourself in the eye. The policewoman who'd locked me up came back to the cell. She gave me a strange look. She must have been thinking, You didn't look like that when I locked you up. She led me out of the cell and

I got ready to hear the worst. What I heard was, they were dropping the charges.

Someone must have explained why I'd got into a fight with this guy. What they said to me was, 'We hear you're going for your first world record in May.'

I said, 'That's right.'

'And you're doing it for charity, aren't you, Paddy? Raising money to help a lad.'

'That's right.' There'd been an article in the *Birmingham Evening Mail* about my record attempt. The police officers had a collection for me.

Then one of the officers said to me, 'Anyway, the bloke you hit is nothing but a wanker. He's on probation and, as a police officer, he's not going to make the grade.' Turns out the guy wasn't just unpopular with me. And then some officers drove me to the hospital to get my black eye looked at, for the record. I didn't tell them I'd punched myself.

CHAPTER 7

TO SURVIVE IS TO WIN

MY FIRST TWO RECORD attempts were for charity. But I soon had to give that up and support myself. I had to eat. I had to live. I sent regular sums to Cancer Research and other UK charities but I wasn't really a fund-raiser. I was an athlete. After that I became more professional. One or two companies started to sponsor me and I saw record breaking as a way to earn some pocket money. I had a full-time job and I had companies helping me with my record attempts. But the extra money only ever paid for my trainers and my food.

When I look back, I've had good times and bad times, like everyone else. But if your career is about challenging world records, the lowest times can be when you can't find a sponsor. So often in the past, I've had to finance myself. It's frustrating when you know you're up for an event that would make good TV. But, not being in a mainstream sport category, I had to fight to get publicity. There are fashions in sport and sponsorship directors don't always notice the changes that are taking place. Financing was a struggle for me from the beginning to the end.

Sponsorship came partly through contacts and partly through being approached by people who wanted to support me. Businesses were happy if I put a poster up behind me while I was challenging a record. For one particular record attempt I did in the Midlands, a guy promised me a certain amount of money to pay my expenses. But, after I'd broken the record, the cash wasn't forthcoming. So I told him I'd be coming round to collect the money in a week's time. I did. And he happened not to be there. I think someone had warned him that, if he didn't pay me, I was the type of person that would put him over a fence. A week later I went round again. He still wasn't there. But he'd left an envelope with one of his staff. I got my money in the end.

But it was frustrating. You're working your guts out and someone says lightly they can't pay you and can you ring them later. You ring later and they're not there. And you're thinking, Right, something's going to happen here. Sometimes a third party would intervene and tell the guy Paddy Doyle was going to sort him out. I'm not a guy to cross or owe money to.

In November 1989 I left my job with the Housing Department so that I could concentrate full time on record attempts. I took part-time jobs to keep the wolf from the door, just agency temping, from admin work in offices to door work and security work. I did warehouse work and casual hours. I was earning a crust, but they were lean years. I knew that if I was going to make a career out of record breaking, I'd have to opt for a lower income. I had to work fewer hours and put more hours into training. I continued to get a small amount of sponsorship from firms who'd supply me with food and sportswear, and that helped a lot. But it was difficult to get that kind of support and it was down to me to find people who would back me.

I'd turn up on Fridays at some firm for a cheque and I'd feel like a debt collector. But it was mostly friends who had their own companies who supported me really. There was a popular newsagent in the Midlands who sponsored me for about eight months. That was a welcome contribution. When I got a sponsor I felt obliged to perform well for them but, in the end, it was business. They'd give me a cheque and I'd put their name on my T-shirt. I reckoned they got their money's worth out of me, large and small companies alike. They got TV and radio coverage out of it. That's the way it is, and you move on.

I was always looking for the next sponsor and planning the next record attempt. It was a business and, as an athlete, I had to be selfish. I had to go for the next record, think about number one. I had to be ruthless with my training. And, when it came to my training partners, I had to push them as much as they pushed me. They got the best out of me in that way.

Another friend, Danny Ryan, helped me a great deal with my record attempts in the last four or five years of my career. He gave me not only support and advice but also sound management. He helped me schedule my time. Paul Jones was another pal who helped me out for a very long time. He took over from John McBean and became my assistant coach at my gym in Erdington. Paul was very loyal and supportive and one hundred per cent behind me. He took over the paperwork for the record attempts and we trained together. He was very good at organising events for me.

I was lucky: Desi and John, then Paul. All these men had something they could give me: their knowledge and experience. They knew me so well. They knew when I was struggling with my training. They knew when to step in. And when I was down they knew how to support me and motivate me. They could read me like a book.

These men were skilled in looking for the warning signs. They knew if my concentration was going while I was sweating and running or punching or kicking. They'd say certain words to help me get a grip on things and get me back on track. This was extremely valuable. Having a team around you when you're faltering can make all the difference. It can get you back up again. During a record attempt I'd listen to what they were saying. I'd block out the noise of the crowd and get on with the job. The voices of my team were the only ones that penetrated. I was tuned in to them. We were professionals in this. I knew their voices so well. I could respond to them in a very positive way.

Boxing, weightlifting and running were the sports I was concentrating on at the time and I combined these with circuit training to prepare for different records. Circuit training is a combination of sit-ups, press-ups, squat thrusts, burpees and shuttle sprints. A squat thrust is a press-up position where you bring your knees up into your chest and kick them back out again. This exercise is particularly good for your legs, the quads, the calf muscles and your thighs.

'Burpee' is an odd name. It sounds more like a bad curry than an exercise. A burpee is a combination of two disciplines: a standing squat, followed by a squat down to your hands and knees, then you kick your feet back out again into a press-up position, bring them back in again and, finally, stand up and jump. Very good for all-round strength and stamina. It's a very demanding discipline and you can find records for it in *The Guinness Book of World Records*. The record I beat was held by two record holders, Ashrita Furman and Pat Docherty, and was listed in the 'Strength and Speed' section. It was a very tough one to do.

I started looking at different books to see which records I could go for. I was always checking to see if I could beat another athlete's time or total. There was a team event, a marathon race where the contestants had to run with a forty-pound weight on their backs. But I didn't have a team I could enter with, so I asked the Guinness people, 'What about setting an individual record for that?' It was soon set up and, in 1988, I ran the Wolverhampton Marathon with a forty-pound backpack in four hours and fifty-six minutes. Later on I set a new record when I ran the London Marathon with the same weight on my back.

My record attempts were in the minority sports bracket and probably still are today. But strength and endurance record events are getting more popular all the time. They are being recognised as up-and-coming sports. Twenty or thirty years ago this kind of sport was virtually ignored. The companies with the money were only interested in tennis, football, cricket and the other main sports.

But society has changed and people are looking for more unusual events to interest them. A couple of decades ago the marathon was enough. Now it's Ultra Marathons, where they do something like a twenty-mile swim, a twenty-mile bike ride and rock climbing. Some of these Ultra Endurance events get TV exposure and the records that are set go into the books.

A phrase I once heard from a competitor in an Ultra Marathon Challenge was: 'To survive is to win.' This particular marathon is a gruelling twenty-day affair where participants have to run, ski and rock climb. What the guy was saying, in effect, was that everyone who finished that course was a winner. I believe Ultra has other endurance events, like ten-mile runs and ten-mile bike events or mountain climbing. But I think these are expensive to enter because you have the top officials, supervisors and medics and stop-off points. It's mostly big companies that enter teams. That's where you need sponsorship.

I never really talked to other competitors in an event until the competition was over. Everyone was more relaxed then, and we'd network a bit. But most athletes I came across weren't interested in going the extra mile in a contest. They were happy to limit themselves to a hundred metres, or whatever. I wasn't going to learn anything from that. I was more interested in fighters: athletes who kept going when the chips were down. I didn't often come across people like that. But when I did, they got my respect.

* * *

Pub landlords were another source of sponsorship. They used to look after me by giving me free meals. But sponsorship was always at grass-roots, spit-and-sawdust level. It was never the multinational corporations that sponsored me, even though I was training as hard as some of the top footballers, and probably ten times harder than some. And they were on £100,000 a week and I was getting a pub meal and twenty-five quid off the pub landlord.

I was breaking world records in the *Guinness Book* and suffering behind the scenes. I was in the newspaper as a role model, getting good write-ups in the *Birmingham Evening Mail* and being interviewed on the radio, on BRMB and WM, but no one knew how hard it was to keep going financially. I was still having to do door work and escort business people to banks, making sure they didn't get mugged.

I also worked for some underworld business barons. I'd accompany them when they were taking money somewhere, either sitting in the car with them or following close behind. These organisations knew I was switched on, being ex-military. I knew what I was looking for and could use my military skills in close-protection work. I was more than muscle or brawn; I knew what I was doing. I was already trained.

Most of my security work at this time came by word of mouth. It's only recently that I've become involved in security at an instructor's level. It was the same with the door work: that came by word of mouth too. Someone would say to himself, 'Paddy's a good doorman. We'll put him out front tonight.' I did door work, on and off, at different venues for about eleven years, from the age of seventeen up until I was twenty-eight. That's long enough for me. It was casual rather than regular work. But door work is hard: verbal and physical confrontations. You have to smile and keep your eyes peeled all the time. It's tough, demanding work, but it's also challenging. I admire anyone who does doors today. They're professionals now. They're licensed and there are inspectors who go around checking on them. I did security work after my late twenties and a few one-offs looking after doors, but I'd basically had enough. My career was taking me in a different direction.

When I was working the doors, it was all about muscle. If anybody argued with you, you could get rid of them. Now, the idea of a doorman has changed. They're called door supervisors and they have to be council-registered. These people have to go on local government courses to learn emergency first aid and customer service. They're now a selling point for a pub or a club, which is good.

Doors in my day? Well, the biggest crooks were doing it. They'd just come out of prison. Now, if you have a criminal record, you can't do a door. Back then, I suppose, doormen did cause friction. I had one confrontation on a door when some lads wanted to come in. There was a short exchange of views and I hit one of them. One of the other doormen restrained me, to stop me going further. About a week later another incident occurred in the same place. A gang of lads wouldn't move on. They were taking their time leaving after time had been called. So I took their beers off the bar and poured them down the sink behind it and told them to get out.

The group started getting verbal towards me and, when they got outside, they were still giving me lip. There was a gang of them there and I was with one other doorman. I went for one of them, struck him and put him on his backside. Admittedly, I was out of bounds there. But that was about nine or ten years ago and I was on a shorter fuse in those days. I just went for the jugular, without thinking. A week later the gaffer's got no one coming in his wine bar. I turn up on the door, as usual, and he says, 'I've got no money tonight for you, Paddy.'

I said, 'Well, I still need paying.' So I went inside and took the money from the till and walked out. I was a bit ruthless then. But, of course, there was no one in the wine bar because I'd scared them all off the week before. I was out of control in those days.

At that time I had some other confrontational business hanging over me from a rugby club I'd been coaching in the Midlands. In the space of three months I'd had two physical confrontations and this verbal one with the gang. The police were running out of patience with me.

One of the players at the rugby club had come up to me after a match and got very abusive. I was part of the coaching staff and he headed for me to let off steam. Next thing I knew, he'd put a pint glass under my nose and pressed it into my face. Well, I warned him, 'If you do that again, I'm going to get very angry.' He went away. Then he came back and did it again, putting the pint glass under my nose. I said, 'Do that again, and we're gonna go outside. I've had enough of this.'

The guy came up to me again and I said, 'Right, let's go outside.' He took his pint glass with him. I knew my capabilities but, to give him a chance, I let him stand on the steps, above me, outside the exit door at the back of the club. I told him, 'Do that again and I'm going to rip your head off.' A lot of people would have hit him, there and then, but I let him go back inside the club.

The fourth time this guy came up to me with the glass and pushed it in my face, I said, 'That's it, outside.' And he brought his pint glass with him again. He told me I wasn't training the team properly and he wasn't scared of me. He could have glassed me; he'd already threatened me verbally and put the glass underneath my face. I found out later he was known as a bit of a bully boy in the club and thought he was a hard man. He'd actually beaten up some of his own team mates.

I told him, 'I've warned you three times. Now I'm going to hit you.' I just hit him. Bang! Knocked him out with the first punch. Cracked his cheekbone. I had to leave him there because there was blood everywhere, all over the ground and my shirt. A friend of mine, one of the committee members, came out and surveyed the scene and said, 'Go, Paddy! Go! We'll look after this.'

I got into the car and headed for the nearest police station to tell them what had happened. I explained I'd been threatened with a glass. The officer on duty at the time didn't seem all that interested, even though I had blood on my shirt. I was told they'd had no complaints, as yet, so they'd leave it at that. OK, I said, and left.

During the week I had a call to say the guy had been telling everyone at the hospital that I'd hit him with a baseball bat. I hadn't. I'd got him with a left hook. It probably felt like a baseball bat. The week after that, while I was working at a local wine bar, the chairman of the rugby club, whose son I still see now and again, came in to see me. I said to the chairman, 'I'll go up before the committee and explain what happened. I'll do everything above board.'

On the Sunday a police officer came round to the wine bar to have a chat with me. And he made sense. What he said was, the guy I'd hit had turned up at the cop shop with his brothers and his dad, saying, 'Paddy Doyle hit me with a baseball bat.' I think the reply he got was something along the lines of, 'Listen, you've been causing problems in the locality for a number of years. You've been a bit of a bully boy. Somebody's come down and put some manners on you, and you can't take it.'

It seems this guy was trying to make out I'm some kind of six-foot-six giant. The officers thought I must be a really big bloke until they saw me, the week after, at another venue where I was running the door. They were surprised. One of the officers said to me something like, 'Paddy, we've sorted out the problem. Now do yourself a favour. You're getting a reputation as an athlete. You're a role model in the press. You're doing the doors. But you aren't doing yourself any favours with a confrontation like that. We don't want people like you. If you continue this kind of behaviour around here, we're going to make it hard for you. We'll stop your car and a few other things.'

So I had to leave my job at the wine bar and the rugby club, which was a bit of a setback. But the partings were amicable. And that guy deserved what he got, I'll stand by that. A couple of weeks later some of the players at the club came up to me and one said, 'Paddy, we're pleased about what you did. That guy banged my head on the pavement once.' A lot of the team were happy about what I'd done. The guy had a mouth and had turned on others. Apparently he was a Jekyll and Hyde character, and turned nasty after a drink or two. I say, what goes around, comes around. Another bully boy got what he deserved. He was the casualty, but he was a casualty who'd asked for it. The only thing that browned me off was having the guy's blood on my shirt. I've seen him since then, with a group of his friends in a hotel bar. He didn't hang around long. He saw me and left very quickly.

I moved on, staying out of the area for a while and focusing on my next record attempt. And I continued doing my record attempts at different venues from 1988 to 1991. It's part of the proof of the record, doing it in public. You can't just do the event in a garage; you've got to go round different locations, as well as doing records in different gyms. I went to various sporting venues, taking part in strength and fitness shows organised by *Strength Athlete* magazine. Unfortunately the magazine isn't published any more. They put on various shows around the country, from Leeds to Southend, and we arranged other events ourselves in Birmingham.

The strength and fitness shows were a combination of power lifting, weightlifting, bodybuilding and other fitness events. They were very popular, and it's a shame no one runs them now. At that time they were a new thing, but I think they'd have a large following now. The public enjoy different types of challenges and events. Just look at how the categories have grown in *The Guinness Book of World Records* in the last ten or twelve years. There used to be three or four lines about karate and judo, but now the book has a whole page on the martial arts. And there are a lot more strength and fitness categories too.

The strength shows included a lot of power lifters and martial artists and strong men. I have a lot of respect for the strong men. They're hard workers. In strong-man competitions, they do a whole range of events. And that's tough; that's hard. I'm not a strong man, I'm an endurance athlete, but I've met one or two genuine strong men, like Jamie Reeves, who's a former World's Strongest Man, and some others, and these men work hard and they're good lads. We talk the same language.

There are certain athletes who get above themselves. Their feet aren't on the ground. Me, I've always been down to earth. I'm still Paddy, and I go into the local and have a jar. I know some guys who've got five world records and they've got above themselves. I've got over a hundred national, European and world records and I'm still me. I haven't changed. I'm still working class, still trying to earn a buck.

Like me, those strong guys have had to do different jobs to keep the money coming in. If you ever see one of those strong-man events, you'll see what they have to go through: about ten events, pulling trucks and lifting weights. I admire these people because they're versatile. A lot of the sports that are coming in now have that variation. Mainstream sports are one thing: cricket bat and ball; football, eleven players. But there are new sports now that attract the eye, like the strong-man events and world-record events like mine. I like the way these sports are developing. I think it's better for all sports.

In this country the martial arts are still in a minority category as a sport. But if you saw the statistics for how many people are coming through the door now to learn them, you'd see they're a lot higher than for tennis or cricket. Friends of mine run martial-arts clubs and they've got forty children in a class. You wouldn't get that at a tennis or cricket club; not forty children joining at the same time. So I think these new sports are under-represented by the Sports Council and other government bodies.

A couple of years ago I had a meeting with the Midlands sports and leisure body. A couple of guys there didn't like kickboxing and they put a spanner in the works to stop the sport being promoted. The Sports Council shouldn't have listened to them because they had no experience of the martial arts. They just didn't like the look of the tournaments, wanting to know if there was proper first-aid back-up. I think they were biased, but it shows how much power people at the top have over a sport.

Rumour can be stronger than fact. However intelligent people are, they tend to believe a rumour. No matter how much experience I've had in life, if someone said to me, 'Stay away from that bloke, he's a thief,' I'd naturally be wary of him. And the comment may be untrue, but you can't test every theory yourself; you have to take on board what others say. But what people say isn't always true. And that's a shame when it involves a sport that I enjoy.

* * *

Every time I went for a world record, I was always in at the deep end straight away. In my sports disciplines there were no pre-competitions, no heats, no rounds, unlike in football or badminton. If you were going for a world record, you were in the hot seat right away. No build-up. It took some time to get used to that. You were in at the top and you had to go for the top, first time round.

And I always took the hard route. I never went for a normal boxing or martial-arts tournament of five minutes or three minutes. I went for four hundred and sixty rounds in one month, challenge events like that. Fitness endurance athletics is the toughest of all the sporting categories. I wanted to do something extra, more than the mile. I wanted to find out what I was made of, push it to the max, achieve the ultimate.

A lot of my records are being broken by athletes now. But not all my records. There isn't one athlete who can break all of my records. I've heard one or two of them say, 'Well, I've beaten Paddy Doyle.' But they haven't really. They'd have to break one hundred and fourteen records to do that. These athletes have specialised in one record, whereas I've broken a range of records in different disciplines. I've seen one or two press cuttings saying athletes have broken one of the records I've set or beaten. But to equal me, they'll have to do the other events and break the other world records, give them to *The Guinness Book of World Records* twenty times plus, then get back to me.

What I've had to do in life is to survive. And part of that survival has meant finding finance for my record attempts. The problem has always been: where do I get the money from? Business people I've known have come to me and said, 'Paddy, I've got a problem. Can you collect some money for me? Can you make sure he doesn't rip us off again?' So I'd go along on behalf of interested parties and tell these people what to do, but I wasn't doing anything wrong or getting into trouble. I was being clever. And I've had doorman agencies coming to me for advice when they've had trouble. It's wheels within wheels. I said I was happy to help them solve their problems, as long as I got money up front. That money went towards my record attempts, and in return I'd put their name on my T-shirt.

But there was a time when I used to act tough for people. I've learnt the hard way. I'm in a minority sport and to survive is all about finance. Without the money, you can't do record attempts. That means, sometimes, you have to do things you maybe feel you shouldn't do. I don't mean sell drugs. I'm not into drugs. I'm too clean for that, too switched on. But I'd do physical work for these guys. And, in return, I'd get a fee or sponsorship.

People don't know what goes on behind the cameras, or behind the name on the T-shirt. There's a lot more to a record attempt than meets the eye. Athletes, at any level now, can receive money. The amateur status has been dropped in sport. They've got professional tennis players in the Olympics. It opens up sport to a wider market.

Society is changing and so is the idea of sport. Twenty years ago the triathlon – run, swim, bike – was looked at as a crazy feat of endurance. Now it's an Olympic sport. Society wants different types of sports these days. People are sick and tired of always looking at cricket and tennis and golf. They want something else.

There are fashions in sport. What I did was fitness and

endurance athletics: a combination of different events. Even the top sports companies, like New Balance, are sponsoring fitness challenges around the UK. There are events like Britain's Fittest Man, which combines about ten different events, including rowing, press-ups and circuit training. So you can see the way tastes are changing. The sports companies realise there's a market for these events now. It wasn't like that when I started out. Whether or not I've helped to popularise fitness and endurance, I don't know, but I know I've inspired others to take up the challenge.

People come up to me and say, 'I've entered a fitness competition, something like your world record challenges. You're the one who inspired me to go in for this.' Whether or not the marketing companies have picked up on this, I don't know. But one fitness company in the UK, who set up a fitness challenge event a couple of years ago, asked me to come along so they could pick my brains on how to demonstrate certain exercises, how they should be done and what the rules are. Two months later they used this in a sports magazine and a fitness competition. In return the company sponsored my own events, so I made a return on it.

I know from experience that anyone who's got a medal for contact sports remembers the event for the lumps and bumps he got winning it. Other athletes may get a hamstring injury or tennis elbow, but the kind of training I needed to do to break records in endurance and the martial arts was tough in the extreme.

Training is where the blood, sweat and tears take place. On the day I went for a world record hardly anyone knew about the preparation that had gone on beforehand, but it was a vital part of it. A training session might typically include a mile run, fifty one-arm press-ups with each arm, ten or fifteen minutes on a punchbag, then I was in the ring, sparring. My head was red with bruises, bumps and lumps. My training was like this for fifteen or sixteen years: tough, demanding, punching and kick pads. I had to include different sports to competition level in my schedule.

In February 1990 the BBC's *Midlands Today* filmed one of my World Record Squat Thrust record attempts in Birmingham. By then I'd already been in *The Guinness Book of World Records* eight times. The TV people interviewed me before the event and asked me how I trained for such an exhausting record. I gave them some idea, then they filmed me doing the attempt. The commentator likened the squat thrusts to a frog's leaping actions. About half an hour into the record attempt, after seven hundred and fifty thrusts, the commentator turned to the camera and said I was looking tired. I still had one thousand, two hundred and sixty squat thrusts to go, just to equal the world record. Forty-five minutes into the attempt, I was up to one thousand, six hundred and eighty thrusts. I started to put pressure on myself, pushing myself to the limit.

By then the commentator couldn't help wondering if I was going to make it. He told the viewers he thought I must have a heart as strong as an ox. He was getting exhausted just watching me. But I wasn't about to let myself or anyone else down. On the hour I'd done two thousand, one hundred and fifty squat thrusts. A new world record. A new world champion.

* * *

For one of my appearances on *Record Breakers*, which was compèred by Roy Castle and Cheryl Baker, I ran a record-breaking mile in the studio on a treadmill machine. It was an athletic endurance record attempt and I had to carry a rucksack full of sand on my back. Before the attempt I was interviewed outside the Wood Lane studios in Shepherd's Bush, London, by one of the compères. Back inside the studio, the athlete David Moorcroft was there to talk the audience through the event. My team were assembled around the machine, ready to do what was necessary to keep me going and on time.

The tension behind the scenes for this kind of programme is palpable. One of the acts before mine was giving the TV staff a headache because they wanted everyone running around after them. They got a bit above themselves apparently. But the BBC seemed to think my record attempt was more important. Meanwhile I was in my dressing room, punching the walls, swearing and getting worked up. Desi Clifton was trying to calm me down. It was my first time on *Record Breakers* and I was understandably nervous about what I had to go out and do in front of the cameras. It was national television, the real thing.

Roy Castle came into the dressing room and saw my state of nervous tension. 'Calm down,' he said to me. 'Just take your time and go for it. Block everything else out.' He knew it was a big event for me and he spent five or ten minutes talking to me. Basically he said, 'Don't go ballistic. Save your energy.' And I took his advice. I was recreating in the studio a one-mile run with a forty-pound backpack. Cheryl Baker pointed out to the audience that I held more stamina records than any other Briton at that time. I was psyched up and ready to go.

The previous day I'd come down to London to do a practice run on the machine for the BBC sound engineers. At one point I went to the toilet and there was a small guy standing there. I didn't clock who it was because I was looking straight ahead. Well, I must have looked strange in my tracksuit top and shorts, so I said to the guy, 'Don't worry, mate, I'm not a fucking weirdo.'

And Bruce Forsyth turned to me and said something like, 'I'm not worried. This place is full of fucking weirdos!'

The programme opened with me doing my 'run-up' on the treadmill, building up speed for the start. The clock started, and I was off. I had to complete the run in under eight minutes and fifteen seconds. The machine duplicated exactly road-running conditions. It showed how far I'd run and the time I'd taken. It gave the speed I was running at, and even the number of calories I was using up. After thirty-six seconds, I was clocking up 7.8 miles an hour and I'd used 13.3 calories. The figures were going to rise a lot after that. Quarter-mile laps were marked on the machine, and I knew I had to run four of those. A light blinked on the panel, indicating the pace of the record I was trying to beat. The machine showed I was ahead. I was determined to stay ahead and get that record.

The compère, Cheryl Baker, was talking to me, asking me how I was feeling. But I couldn't hear her. I was focused on my record attempt, one hundred per cent. Roy Castle introduced David Moorcroft, the five-thousand-metres record-breaker, and he took over the commentating while I kept running. Roy said to David, 'You know what it's like to keep up this kind of pace, don't you?'

The athlete replied, 'I know what it's like to run a mile, but never with forty pounds on my back. That really is hard. And it's going to get harder and harder as the running goes on.' He told the audience, 'It's difficult to stay on a treadmill at the best of times, but Paddy's exercised twice a day for this: a combination of weight training and running.'

I had my team standing by. Desi Clifton, my trainer, and Dave, my nutritionist, were there, and they controlled the speed I was running at. I'd started off reasonably steadily. Later I got Desi to change the speed, so I could run faster and beat the record.

I'd started well. I was on the maximum speed already. If I kept up the pace, I'd finish the mile in under seven minutes. After two minutes, thirty-nine seconds, I was running at eight miles an hour. That was well inside my schedule. They expected me to drop off a bit when I got on to the third lap and go faster and run harder when I knew I was on the last lap. David Moorcroft could see the concentration in my face. He realised I was hardly aware they were all standing round me under the studio lights. But he knew I'd need the support at the end.

The record I was trying to beat was my own record. But it wasn't the only record I held at the time. I had nineteen world records for strength and endurance events. I'd done two thousand, two hundred and seventy-five squat thrusts in an hour and I'd done seven thousand, seven hundred and forty-three one-arm press-ups in five hours. David Moorcroft explained to the audience how difficult one-arm press-ups were to do. I'd done five thousand sit-ups with a fifty-pound weight on my stomach, and thirty-seven thousand, three hundred and fifty press-ups in twenty-four hours. What I wanted to do now was get into *The Guinness Book of World Records* more times than anyone else. And I was well on my way.

Roy Castle mentioned the dramatic races David Moorcroft had run in his time. 'Which of those records of Paddy's would you rather not try?' he asked him.

David said, 'One of the most amazing records Paddy did, and he took a whole year to do it, was when he did an average of four thousand press-ups every day, which made a total of 1,500,230 press-ups. And he needed a witness for every single press-up.' Meanwhile I was continuing my run on the treadmill at nine miles an hour.

I had been interviewed earlier by Cheryl Baker about how I went about my training. She pointed out that I was a true 'record breaker', with nineteen records under my belt. Then she asked me how I set about getting into such an incredible career. I told her I'd been involved in competitive sports from the age of eight and, over the years, this interest had strengthened. I said that when I came out of the army I decided to channel my physical and sporting abilities into breaking world records and, at the same time, raise money for a number of charities.

'But there are lots of ways to raise money for charities. Why break records?' Cheryl asked me. I told her I was trying to beat the thirty world endurance records held by Ashrita Furman of the USA. She said that Ashrita had been on *Record Breakers* several times and that they had spoken to him about my record attempts. Ashrita said he was amazed at what I was doing and that he admired me. I took that as a real compliment.

Cheryl then took a look at the backpack I'd be carrying while I was on the treadmill. She could hardly lift it. She found it incredible that I would be running a mile with this pack full of sand. She wanted to know if there was anything special about the sack. I explained it was just an ordinary army backpack with sand inside, taped up so that it would hold together while I was running on the machine. Cheryl said it must be like giving someone a piggyback for a mile run.

She asked how I trained for a record-breaking event. I told her it depended on the event, but it normally involved training for two hours in the morning and two hours in the evening. 'What keeps you going?' she asked.

I shook my head and smiled. 'I don't know really,' I said. 'At the end of the day, I like a challenge. I believe I can push myself beyond certain barriers. When pain gets to you, at the end of the day, it's the mind that controls the body.'

'But there must be a limit,' Cheryl insisted.

'I don't actually think so,' I told her. 'If your body's fit and your will is strong, you can do anything you put your mind to.'

And there I was, coming up to the end of my mile. I knew I had the energy left to go faster. I raised my arm to signal Desi to speed up the treadmill. Faster. Faster. I was on my last lap. I was doing well at nine miles per hour. But it was hard now. You could see it on my face. The crowd were cheering and whistling. I had one-tenth of a mile to go. I'd taken six minutes, twenty seconds. They could see my legs were getting tired, but I maintained my pace. I was way ahead of the record. And I passed the mile in six minutes, fifty-six seconds.

The applause was deafening as the machine was stopped. I staggered off with the backpack. 'Unbelievable,' said Roy Castle.

'A fabulous performance,' said David Moorcroft.

I raised my hands to acknowledge the applause of the studio audience. 'Thank you very much everybody.'

Roy said, 'Our thanks to Paddy. You've given us this world record. A very exciting one indeed. Thank you very much.'

And the programme ended with the song 'Dedication, that's what you need …'

CHAPTER 8

FIT TO FIGHT

THERE ARE QUITE a few categories in the martial arts. There's judo and karate, kickboxing and tai-kwando, kumite sparring and western self-defence. Western self-defence is a combination of ground/floor grappling, karate and boxing. It's designed for the street. You can adapt this discipline to different environments; that's the best thing about western self-defence. Some martial arts can only be adapted to the mat and need a referee. In a street scenario, a confrontation happens differently. Western self-defence is useful because it involves more explosive power moves. You use a combination of different strikes for different parts of the body. Not for attacking, but for defending yourself. You've got to be legal about this.

The martial arts are a form of endurance sport, but they're more about hard contact than other fitness and endurance events. Most martial-arts organisations give you your dans after you've got your third dan, rather than assess you, because they're awarded for knowledge and experience. You don't go through an examination. You know your techniques and fighting skills after a number of years of practising. But, for my fourth dan from the Spirit Combat Association in 2000, I insisted on doing a number of rounds of fighting, rather than just receive the dan. I don't like to feel I've received an award without earning it. I'm a great believer in sweating for something. So they put me through a hard test.

In 2001 I worked for my fifth dan. This time I chose to do twenty rounds of full-contact fighting, twenty rounds of semi-contact fighting, a ten-mile run and one thousand press-ups, all of which were witnessed and recorded by club members. Then, when I went up north to get the dan, I was assessed again, this time by the Self Defence Federation International, as a kind of double check. By going through all these assessments, I felt I'd earned my fifth dan.

The president of the Self Defence Federation International, Dave Turton, has become a good friend of mine. But he doesn't do me any favours and I respect him for that. Everyone in his association goes through the same rigorous testing. Dave is a black belt, seventh dan, and has a lot of experience in self-defence.

Another guy I look up to is Professor Brian Dossett, who's a black belt, tenth dan. His organisation, the Spirit Combat Association, is based in Woking, Surrey, a very nice part of southern England, where I went for my fourth dan.

I'm also a second dan with the World United Martial Arts

Association, or WUMA. This is probably the toughest organisation for gradings: they put you through pain and back. And that's what they did with me when I went for my second dan. It was two days of hard physical work.

I owe a lot to Richard Hopkins, the president of WUMA. He's been very supportive over the years and has become a great friend. Richard is a former top martial-arts fighter. He decided to set up his own association, which now has over twenty thousand members worldwide. The organisation is based at Charlton Kings, in Cheltenham. Recently the Association held their annual World Martial Arts awards and presented me with a trophy for Best All Round Athlete of the Year. They said I was a good ambassador for the association and the sport, and I was very honoured to receive the award. It's the Oscars of the martial-arts world.

I fully respect these men, Dave Turton, Brian Dossett and Richard Hopkins. I've gained a lot of specialised knowledge from them, along with the support of Desi Clifton, and they've each helped me in different ways to get to world-record level. I've been on their advanced courses as an instructor and I've been assessed by their gradings. They've put me through it and made me think about the theory as well as the physical skills.

I strongly believe that if you're a martial-arts instructor, it's a good thing to join different associations and learn various styles and techniques. It improves your own skills and you're able to pass on a good variety of techniques to your students. For self-defence on the street today, you need to know as many different approaches as possible. Thirty years ago hardly anyone carried knives or CS gas. Now, society has changed and you have to be prepared for new forms of aggression.

I joined the World United Martial Arts Association in 1994. I already had my judo skills from childhood and my fourteen years' amateur boxing experience, which started in my teens. I'd come out of the army and begun to challenge world records and was concentrating on boxing and judo workouts. Then I saw a course being advertised in a martial-arts magazine and, in April 1994, I went on an instructor's course in freestyle martial arts. 'Freestyle' means a combination of everything, from karate to weapons training. Weapons training involves defence skills: what to do if someone comes at you with a knife or a piece of wood.

The course was held in Cheltenham and lasted a day. I found I enjoyed the sport and decided to go for the grades. Apart from weapons training, we learnt about safety and refereeing. A lot of it was new to me but I could apply the skills I already had. I was familiar with punching and kicking techniques in judo. I wasn't a complete novice and I adapted well to the martial arts. I really enjoyed it. It was something different. I felt I'd learnt enough from boxing and I wanted to look at another side of fighting. Not everyone can make the transition from boxing to the martial arts.

WUMA is an excellent organisation. It's like a family, and I felt an immediate camaraderie. I realised I was in a good set-up and I could start at a basic level. I was able to learn in a solid fashion as I went through my gradings for my belts, from yellow onwards. As I said, today I'm a black belt, second dan. The higher dans come with age and you're normally well into your fifties and sixties when you get to the tenth dan. It's not just about physical fitness at that stage; it's also knowledge and experience. You're like a guru at that level: highly respected.

You start with the basic stretching techniques: the punching and the kicking. There are also fitness workouts, such as press-ups, to build your general strength and stamina. And you're constantly assessed; it's an ongoing thing. You learn angle kicks and how to put power into your kicks and punches, how to use the whole of your body.

There were people on the course from all walks of life, both male and female. A lot of women are coming into the sport these days. They're more interested in freestyle martial arts now than in fitness and endurance. They're moving away from step and aerobics; they want something else. They want to get on to the mat and fight, put a suit on and go for gradings. Both men and women want something different in sport now, and they don't want to see the traditional sports on TV all the time.

I began teaching basic unarmed combat in 1994. I called the course 'Fight to Survive' and it included fitness training for stamina and basic boxing skills, as well as unarmed combat techniques I'd learnt in the Paras. But my courses had much more breadth and depth once I'd registered with those three martial-arts associations. And once you've gained your black belt and you have the knowledge to instruct properly, you can get full liability insurance for teaching. It's an all-round stamp of approval.

My courses are evolving all the time as I take on board new knowledge and continue to go on courses myself. I love to learn new techniques; there's so much out there to absorb. And I get so much enjoyment passing it all on to my students. But I like to teach realistic unarmed combat in my gym: what works, rather than traditional, outdated self-defence moves. There are a lot of out-of-date techniques still being taught out there.

Realistic techniques include the full-contact kicking moves which work in self-defence. Boxing skills are also important. It depends on your speed, but you can try to punch someone on the jaw or the nose. But without a boxing glove, you have to accept you're going to walk away with a few grazes, maybe broken fingers or knuckles. Judo skills are useful for throwing. You can get hold of someone and throw them to the ground. Ground/floor-grappling moves, a combination of judo and wrestling techniques, are a must. Nine times out of ten a confrontation in a street will end up on the ground. You have to be good with your hands to avoid going down in the first place, but if it happens, you want to be on top.

If someone comes at you with a knife, you can try to kick it out of the way, or use monkey kung fu. When a monkey gets mad, what does he do? He'll pick up things and throw them at you. So, if anyone comes at you with a knife or a baton, look around you and see what you've got on the ground. Pick up a chair, a table or a fire extinguisher to defend yourself. Otherwise you're going to be brown bread, dead.

It's about speed and timing, how much you train and how hard you train. But you have to get it right in the gym before you can get it right in the street. I'm often asked by local government agencies, schools and social workers to teach them self-defence skills. They know I have a broad base of knowledge and experience, and that I've been properly examined and assessed. And I've got competitive experience as well.

WUMA holds a Warlords kumite tournament every two years. For this event, every black belt in the organisation has to fight one hundred rounds to show he's worthy of his grading. It's hard enough to get your black belt and your dans, but WUMA has thrown this event in to keep you up to standard. In May 2000, along with about sixty other dan-grade instructors, I got ready to go to the tournament at the Cheltenham Recreation Centre.

But on the Friday night before the event, Richard Hopkins, WUMA's president, mentioned there was a world record, held by a Canadian, which stood at one hundred and twenty rounds. He asked me if I wanted to go for it. I said I would. Doing one hundred rounds is very tough and demanding on its own, even with a proper break after each round. But going for the record would mean five hours continuously on my feet, and this was at twenty-four hours' notice.

During the tournament my feet were burning. They were covered in blisters from all the punching and kicking. My legs were covered in bruises, so were my shins and my thighs. Every part of your body gets battered in these contests. Every two minutes, you have a different opponent, another kumite instructor. And they're doing the same as you, fighting for their one hundred rounds. But I had to go way above that number to get the world title.

The contest is both mentally and physically demanding. You have to remain switched on and move quickly; you've got to be able to get out of a situation. I had the usual head guard on but my shins were killing me. I knew that if I failed on the hundredth round, I'd have failed completely.

Some of the instructors I came up against were British, European and world champions. They're the highest level of fighters and I fully admire them. It's about all-round fighting ability and mental agility, and a high level of concentration and staying power. But I did it: one hundred and thirty-one rounds for WUMA's Warlords Kumite World Title. And I had to complete them in five hours exactly. I must have lost about four or five pounds in weight.

After receiving the certificate I headed for a hot shower with all the other instructors, then we had some fruit. Everybody was on a high. But I was drained after my extra rounds. It's surprising how much it takes out of you, doing nearly a third as many rounds more than the usual one hundred. And I'd been fighting that much harder because I was going for a record. It took a good week to recover and the bruises took a couple of weeks to go. I took a lot of side shots on my head. I think you can go through a kind of slight concussion afterwards. You're a bit woozy on your feet.

With any sort of contact sport, in boxing and in the martial arts, there's always a question of whether you're going to inflict an injury on someone or what they're going to do to you. It's a risk you have to accept before you go for a high-level dan grade or a tournament. And at a Warlords kumite tournament, anything can happen. Someone could throw a punch and break your nose. There were a few broken noses on that day. I think I contributed to a couple of them. But everyone's a sports professional and shakes hands afterwards.

I'd recommend the martial arts for anyone of any age, including women. There were quite a few dan-grade female instructors at the tournament and they were keen to give as good as they got. The tournament was a new event of its kind for the WUMA instructors and they got a fair amount of media exposure. In addition, the Midlands press picked up on the world record I achieved. When the next Warlords kumite tournament comes round, I'll be retired from world-record competitions but it's tempting to think about going for the record again. I'll always be interested a challenge, especially the Warlords Kumite World Title.

The reason there are so many different branches of the martial arts is that there are a lot of different organisations out there. There are about eight or nine different styles of karate now and each organisation thinks it's got a new system. Kickboxing is a combination of tai-kwando, Thai boxing and karate. I tend to focus on the more traditional unarmed combat: close-quarter self-defence. This can be used not only for defending yourself in the street but also for competitions in the martial arts. It's basic ground/floor grappling, which is a form of wrestling, combined with some karate techniques, boxing and basic judo throws. This gives a student a combination of four different methods of fighting, from a standing position to groundwork.

With boxing, there are only two organisations: the ABA for amateurs and the Professional Boxing Association for the pros. Boxing and sparring records aren't necessarily something you enjoy. They take a lot out of you; they're tough. But there are four or five records I went for in that category that are memorable. One was the WUMA Full Contact British Title Challenge Record, in June 1997, at the BT Sports Hall in Sheldon, in Birmingham. I did two hundred and fifty-one rounds of freestyle martial arts, a combination of karate and kickboxing, over a ten-day period. I started fighting at my own gym, Staminas Self Defence Centre in Erdington, and the grand finale was in Sheldon. On the last day I went sixteen rounds with the top guys, champions. The hall was packed and the fighting was tough. I fought Winston 'Spider' Harris, and that guy can kick. Every time he kicked me, it was like being cut on the side of the head. He's won a lot of titles himself. He's a top martial artist. Another guy, Karl Gibbs, is an excellent fighter and heavyweight karate champion. He'd only heard an hour before the event that he had to fight me. One of his club members called him and asked if he wanted to do it. I've got a lot of respect for someone who can turn out at an hour's notice. And he came at me with a lot of bottle.

In another competition, the British Challenge Boxing Martial Arts Title Record at the Carterton Sports Centre, in Oxford, in February 1999, I had six boxers and martial-arts fighters taking it in turns to fight me, so it was virtually like having a fresh fighter for every round. That was a very hard record to do because of the standard of my opponents. Some were at national level. And those guys came out wanting my blood. One bloke was seven times the national martial-arts kickboxing champion. He came out kicking and punching everywhere. Unbelievable. I did sixteen rounds of full-contact martial arts. The body took a lot of punishment, but I think I lost only three rounds out of the sixteen.

A couple of days after I got the title, I was having blackouts of a sort. I felt dizzy, as though I wasn't there. My head hurt. It had taken a lot of punches and kicks. Full-contact fighting is different from semi-contact or points fighting. In those competitions they just touch people. In full-contact fighting you're going out there to crush bones. I decided not to do any more of those kinds of events after that. I'd proved myself. I'd done my best.

I remember I got a lovely kick on the side of the head. It stung, just as though someone had put a knife in my temple. But the crowd was so supportive that I carried on. Even so, it was tough. Every challenge event in martial-arts boxing is like that. You don't go in there with any easy options. Whatever you're going for, you know you've got to work for it. And you accept that before you go for it. If you can't accept it, you shouldn't be there. I knew that whatever I did, regardless of which event I took on, I was going to walk away with lumps, bumps, bruises, grazes or cuts. I always put one hundred per cent into what I did.

The crowd play a great part in lifting you in challenge events. Not that they were all on my side in boxing or martial-arts competitions. A lot of them were there to support their own club member or friend or brother. I probably attracted a number of people, and I'm sure some of them came to see me lose. I probably had a few enemies out there. All I could say to them was, 'Come along and see me if you've got any problems. Any time.'

The winning and the applause when you're doing a contact sport give you a real buzz, a tension. Whether it's judo or boxing or freestyle martial arts, you don't just get put in for a tournament; you have to go through a pre-selection process at your own club, so you've got to be of a certain standard in the first place.

One of my proudest moments was in August 2001, when I got the Martial Arts Punch Kick Record at the Airborne and Special Forces Show: four thousand, one hundred and four punches and one thousand, five hundred and sixty kicks in one hour. A very interesting event, held each August at Bletchley Park, near Milton Keynes, Buckinghamshire, the show allows retired and serving forces personnel to come together and demonstrate different skills and technology to the public and to other personnel. One of the top generals of recent decades, General Sir Farrar Hockley, presented me with my certificate.

A lot of my boxing records have been combined with the martial arts. I often fight boxers and martial artists alternately. It's called a freestyle full-contact challenge. One of the most memorable of those challenges was in August 1995, when I attempted the European Record Full Contact Fighters Combat Title. I fought five hundred and sixty boxing and martial-arts rounds with different fighters over a period of a month. I was a middleweight then, and I had to find a succession of different fighters to take me on in the lead-up to the grand finale on 24 August. The number of fighters coming at me became eight, then twelve. They just kept coming.

I'd been approached by some martial-arts instructors to go for the title. We knew that American martial-arts fighters had gone for records like this. The Americans had done a certain number of rounds non-stop for a number of hours, but we decided to see what I could do over a period of a month for a European record.

I'd been training normally before the challenge. Boxing and the martial arts are a substantial part of my training programme, even today. I do a lot of freestyle karate. For two months before the challenge, I supplemented these disciplines with a large amount of stamina training in the gym: bag work, skipping and a lot of martial-arts boxing programmes. It was an approach I also used for the kumite titles, which were also non-stop-fighting events. I had to prepare myself to take a lot of punishment. I didn't just go into these events and walk away with a few grazes. I got some serious knocks.

You can adapt your body for the punishment you're going to get by doing sparring sessions in training. During these sessions you're punched and kicked by different sparring partners. Obviously you're not just going to stand there and take it. You move around and your body and mind are prepared for fighting. You develop a mental alertness; you spring and get out of the way. But not everyone's born with the ability to take physical punishment. You've got to want to get up there and do it. There's no way you can be forced into it. You've got to assess the situation and the timing, and get your own punches and kicks in. You get used to being punched and kicked over a period of time. It's a question of learning to ride the kick or the elbow or the punch when you're moving around the ring.

You have to forget about the pain and persevere. It's mind over matter. I've done so much training and fighting over the years that I reckon my bone density is compact enough to withstand a lot of punishment. If you don't have good bone mass, the bones can shatter on impact. But whenever I'm injured, I see my osteopath or sports therapist straight away. I don't let the injury linger and wait for it to repair itself. I was lucky enough to have a team around me when I was competing, but my advice to anyone with an injury is to get it seen to.

The first task for the Full Contact Fighters Combat Title fight in August 1995 was to contact various martial artists around the clubs and find out who'd be able to come down to my gym and fight me. They had to sign a document to say they'd fought with me, and in which rounds. There was a timekeeper there and everything had to be countersigned. There was a referee, Vinny Lee, a former martial-arts kickboxing champion himself, to make sure the rules for the record were properly adhered to. The hall was packed with people. Desi Clifton and Aidan Canavan, a good friend of the family, were my corner men.

The fighting took place every day for a month. I got a few bruises, two black eyes, a broken finger and a broken toe. I carried the broken toe and the broken finger into the finale. My finger

went early in the month, when I was punching, and I cracked a
middle toe when I was giving a forward kick to someone's shin. I
heard the crunch against the other guy's bone. But I delivered my
fair share of injuries as well as quite a few knockouts.

At the finale, out came a fighter I'd fought before at other
boxing and martial-arts challenges. I caught him with a right cross
to the jaw. He went down and took a standing count of nine. To
give him his due, he stood up and came at me again. But I beat
him on points because I'd knocked him down.

There were a lot of punches and kicks and bruises. A lot of pain,
I remember. One journalist wrote that he'd gone along there for a
laugh, to see me getting pulverised by a succession of fighters. He
ate his words, and was certainly impressed, when I won. I'd gone
fifteen full rounds.

But on the final day I wasn't sure I'd get the record. I knew I
was up against it. I was taking on different fighters at different
weights. That was a challenge in itself. I was fighting
middleweights – my own weight – and heavyweights who'd been
in the ring a long time and had a lot of experience. You'd think I'd
only do this kind of challenge once. I didn't. I took this event on
five or six times. I did the Yearly Boxing Sparring Record in 1994,
and that was four thousand and six rounds. In 1995 I took the
Weekly Full Contact Sparring Title. And there was the WUMA
Freestyle Sparring Title in 1996 and the WUMA Full Contact
British Title Challenge record in 1997. Then, in 1999, I took the
British Challenge Boxing Martial Arts Title Record, and in 2000
the Warlords Kumite World Title. Often my record challenges

overlapped; I'd be going for more than one kumite title in the same event. It happened constantly. And that's what I liked: the constant challenge.

I don't spar in my own gym. I prefer to go to a karate club in the area and spar there with the instructors and seniors. It keeps me flexible on the punching and kicking side. In September 2001 I went to an inter-club martial-arts tournament at the Cornerstone Karate Club in Birmingham. I went along there to fight; I just turned up. But they didn't have an opponent for me at my level, so they gave me a line of black and senior coloured belts who were fighting there. There were about seven or eight of them and they were a bit nervous about fighting me, but I fought them in front of the spectators. I was asked to take it easy and not to knock anyone out. I think I won on points.

I've been a martial-arts teacher since 1987. Once you're a black belt you can get full indemnity insurance to teach, as this means you've got the knowledge and expertise to run a course responsibly. But it also takes skill to put your knowledge across, to demonstrate skills. Not everyone can do that. Some have got it and some haven't. I like to motivate people, especially those who want to learn. The greatest test is to teach people who don't want to learn and persuade them that certain skills are going to benefit them.

These days more people than ever are interested in the martial arts. More and more of us have been verbally and physically threatened and more people want to make sure it doesn't happen again. Quite a few people who've come to my classes have been in physical confrontations. One guy phoned me a while back. He said he used to box but he sounded a bit of a nutter. He said he wanted to learn self-defence to beat up his next-door neighbour. I said, 'What's it all about then?'

'Parking his car in front of my car,' he said. 'I don't like it.'

I paused for a moment. I couldn't teach him martial-arts skills for something like that. It'd reflect badly on me.

He said, 'Yeah, but I don't mind going down for it again.'

'What do you mean?'

'I've been sectioned seven times and put in a mental institution. I'll go back there again if I have to.'

I said, 'See ya,' and put the phone down. But he turned up at the gym a couple of times after that. I could see he wasn't the full shilling. I'd have got into trouble for showing him martial-arts techniques. He was an intense sort of guy. Lived with his mother. And he was going to do some damage to the Muslim who lived next door, who was browning him off.

As an instructor, you have to weigh up the motives of those who come to you to learn. If you're a good instructor, your standards are high. You're a sergeant major, a nurse, a counsellor, a team leader. You've got to think fast and solve problems as they arise. When you reach a high dan level, you're expected to be able to use your initiative in teaching. It's part of the responsibility. And you have to wield more discipline in contact sports than you do as a coach in other sports. You can get someone come along who's better at punching and kicking than their opponent. They can take advantage of that, once you've turned your back, by fighting too hard. You've got to be a referee with eyes in the back of your head; you've got to be ready to pull people apart.

The martial arts use a lot more of your body than boxing. You're using your feet and elbows to defend yourself. Boxing is a full-contact sport from day one. But in the martial arts you can practise semi-contact. The sport has given me a lot of self-discipline and confidence. I've made good friends within the martial-arts world and I've also got recognition in the form of awards, which I think shows people's respect for what I've achieved. That's a nice feeling. And the associations I'm connected with have certainly looked after me well.

When I first started learning the martial arts, kicking was completely new to me, and certain individuals tried to take advantage of that. While I was doing my lower gradings, one or two of the instructors were kicking me around the head when I'm sure they knew I only had boxing skills. On one particular grading, I got fed up with it. I had some bad bruises around the head and I wasn't having any more of it. One of my opponents was a black belt, second dan. They were all at a fairly high level. I started using my boxing skills and, bang! I put three of them on their arses, and made them sit it out with concussion or knocked them out.

I looked at the senior examiner there, as if to say, 'Well, it's not my fault. They're kicking me and they know I'm not that good at it.' He said, 'For Christ's sake, don't knock any more of them out. Have a bit of self-control.' I got the grading. But I was warned every time I went for a grading, 'You've got to have more self-control.' My argument was, 'They're knocking shit out of me, so I've got to do something in return.' When I put these fellows down, I think I broke the nose of one of them. I still see some of the blokes today, at various gradings and advanced courses I go to.

I had a lot of aggression in me then, and I still have. But now I've got more control with my kicking and my power, and I'm using all the moves. In a street situation you tend to go back to what you know, but a bit of kicking helps a lot. And I use my forward kicks and my side kicks in the ring when I'm sparring, and for the Warlords kumite tournament. They're good moves to have, because they give your arms a rest.

Once, in the early days, when I was a student on a bodyguard course, there was a guy there who was a brown belt in aikido, which involves kicks and the hands. At the time I was a brown belt in freestyle martial arts, karate and western self-defence. It was a sparring session, which was part of the course, with different students and different instructors. And I didn't have a box on to protect my groin.

This guy was continually aiming at my groin. I told him about it three times, then I reported it to the chief instructor. But the bloke continued kicking in that direction, so I thought, Well, I can't have this, and I punched him in the face. He ended up, so I was told at a later grading, with eight stitches and two teeth missing. He went from the hospital to the dentist. And he complained about it. But I did say I'd warned him three times, and the course instructors stuck up for me.

* * *

Sometimes, when you're in the ring, if you're boxing or sparring, a partner can come in and try to knock you out. That's happened many a time. In the early days, around 1990 and 1991, there was a black guy from Sheffield who used to come down to the gym and spar with me. He used to spar with some of the top names then, professional boxers. He was a good boxer and he'd try to knock me out every time. It took me a long time to fathom out how to get in between his guard. Then one day I got inside and knocked him spark out. Put him on the floor. I never saw him again.

It took me six hard months to achieve this, and I was getting black eyes and cut eyes for my trouble. At the end of the day, I don't think the guy could take it. He didn't know how to handle being put on his backside. He was hurt badly. I'd taken the wind right out of his sails. All those years he'd been used to getting in the ring and giving it out. Suddenly he was on the receiving end. But he'd been punishing me for six months before that. And he was a good partner because he was pushing me; he was getting the best out of me. He knew I was training for these different record attempts. Even then I had perseverance, but for half a year he'd been punishing me. Then I punished him for two minutes and he didn't like it, and I never saw him again. The quality of the athlete always comes through in the end. It's all in the strength of mind.

I've had to use this strength of mind myself on many occasions for defence purposes. You go on automatic pilot if you've been trained properly. If somebody's coming at you, you don't waste time looking at their eyes; you're looking at where you want to aim.

This cuts out going through the freeze mode. You go straight into your stance, looking at what you're going for, whether it's punching or kicking an elbow or a head.

You have to decide quickly what action you're going to take, and that depends on how close your opponent is to you. If they get close enough, you punch. If they're going to kick out, you block it and kick back, or move in quick and punch or strike, or grab legs and bring them down to the floor.

Trouble is, I don't always know my own strength. One night I was out with some members of my gym. We all went down to a nightclub in Birmingham city centre and one of my training partners got caught smoking dope. Fair enough. I don't smoke it myself, but it doesn't mean I dictate to others. The guy said to me, 'Paddy, I've got to go.'

I said, 'Why've you got to go?'

He says, 'I've been caught smoking Bob Hope. The doorman's asked me to leave the club.'

Mind you, I was in a bad mood that evening. I'd had a drink. It was my birthday. I said to the guy, 'Do you want to go, or don't you?'

'No,' he says.

This big black doorman came over to me. I'm not going to mention his name; he's a family man and he's been full of respect for me since then. All the lads with me were black too. It was me and six black lads, all from my gym. Good blokes. As the white guy, I stuck out. I looked like the ringleader.

He must have been six foot four, this doorman, and about

sixteen or seventeen stone. He was a weightlifter, strong and wide. I put my glass down and went for him. Immediately a fight broke out in the club and everybody got involved in the free-for-all. Fair dos to the mates who were with me: when the doormen came at me, one of the lads gave one of them a good hiding and knocked him out.

Meanwhile there was me and this big doorman, grappling on the dance floor. He was trying to punch me in my groin and I had him in a stranglehold. I wouldn't let go. My grip got tighter and tighter. I didn't see the man's face; I wasn't aware of my hand, tight around his throat. I didn't feel the windpipe I was crushing. As my friends dragged me off the bouncer, I saw his tongue projecting from the side of his mouth. Another minute, and he would have been history. And he wouldn't have been the first to have a near-death experience with Paddy Doyle.

John McBean, the former amateur boxer, was with me. He told me later they'd realised if they hadn't pulled me off the doorman, I would have killed him. The guy was already out for the count, but I still hadn't let go of him. I was out of control. I don't know what I would have done. I don't want to think about it. But that was it. The lads and I got out of the club and split up. I said we'd meet up again, but they didn't want to know.

About eighteen months later I was at a martial-arts tournament in Birmingham. I was sitting there, watching the bouts, when there was a tap on my shoulder. I turned round and the guy said, 'You don't remember me, Paddy, do you?'

I looked at the man, sitting there with his wife. 'No,' I said.

It was the big doorman. He said, 'Last time we met, I was on the club floor, out cold.' We looked at each other for a moment.

'Are you all right then?' I asked him.

He said, 'Yeah, it's OK now.' He'd taken it well and accepted what had happened. And he looked a lot leaner and fitter. He'd got more into the cardiovascular mode. He'd lost a lot of weight. I supposed he realised that muscle is more powerful than fat.

And two seats away was another black lad. Someone I'd knocked out in the second round at a martial-arts boxing tournament. And, to the left, there was another guy: a martial-arts champion I'd knocked out in another challenge tournament. Looking round, I suddenly noticed I was surrounded by blokes I'd given a good hiding to. But it was all right. We behaved very respectably and shook one another's hands.

The Iron Man.

Giving it my all in the World Fitness Endurance Challenge.

Top: I ran 0.39 miles in 5 minutes, carrying a 40lb pack on my back.

Bottom: Team Doyle celebrating my 115th world record.

Feeling the heat.

OUT OF THE ASHES: "THEY SHALL MOUNT UP WITH WINGS AS EAGLES."

Western Self Defense

RANK CERTIFICATE

OF THE UNITED STATES MARTIAL ARTS ASSOCIATION

BE IT KNOWN TO ALL MARTIAL ARTISTS THAT

Patrick Daniel J. Doyle

HAS COMPLETED THE REQUIREMENTS FOR THE RANK OF

Fifth Dan

WITH DATE OF RANK OF

January 1, 2001

AND IS OFFICIALLY REGISTERED IN THE NATIONAL RECORDS AS FULLY QUALIFIED IN THIS RANK.

Philip S. Porter, Founder, USMA   Approving Official   Jack A. Carter, Secretary, USMA

OUT OF THE ASHES: "THEY SHALL MOUNT UP WITH WINGS AS EAGLES."

Freestyle Karate Kumite Full Contact

RANK CERTIFICATE

OF THE UNITED STATES MARTIAL ARTS ASSOCIATION

BE IT KNOWN TO ALL MARTIAL ARTISTS THAT

Patrick Daniel J. Doyle

HAS COMPLETED THE REQUIREMENTS FOR THE RANK OF

Fifth Dan

WITH DATE OF RANK OF

January 1, 2001

AND IS OFFICIALLY REGISTERED IN THE NATIONAL RECORDS AS FULLY QUALIFIED IN THIS RANK.

Philip S. Porter, Founder, USMA   Approving Official   Jack A. Carter, Secretary, USMA

My Fifth Dan Certificates.

Top: In Western Self Defense.

Bottom: In Freestyle Karate Kumite Full Contact.

Top: The Full Contact Kumite Karate combat record was 560 rounds in one calendar month. I achieved it in August 1995, at the Holly Lane Sports Centre Birmingham.

Bottom: Winning the Freestyle Kumite Karate monthly sparring record – with 467 Full Contact rounds in 23 days in September 1996.

Top: The Alternate Squat Thrust Record at RAF Cottlesmore.

Bottom: Victorious again!

CHAPTER 9

BEWARE OF SMALL MEN

MARTIAL-ARTS CLUBS are springing up everywhere these days, and it's great to see that. The sport is a good discipline for kids and it builds their confidence. I've personally found the martial arts very useful streetwise. They help you develop an awareness, so that you're always ready for troublesome moments. If someone is deliberately blocking your path, and you do get people like that, you can bump into them, making out it's an accident, give them a bit of an ankle sweep, say, 'Sorry, didn't see you,' and walk on. It puts some manners on them.

In the past I've had trouble with gangs vandalising property near my gym, breaking fence panels and windows. When I've caught them at it, I've used some restraining techniques which don't bruise them but give them the message they're not to do it again. There may be eight or nine of them in a gang but you can't hesitate, you've just got to go in there. I don't want the area around my gym looking like a crap-hole.

Restraining techniques? I usually grab the biggest one in the group by the throat and jab my fingers into his stomach. It's not like a punch; the tips of the fingers go straight into the gut area. You cap it off by projecting your voice strongly. The gang think they're invincible because there are a number of them, but you walk towards the biggest and loudest one first. You're verbalising as you go, giving him a walk-through-talk-through. 'Don't do it again,' bop-bop-bop. It's strike first.

I don't do this sort of thing as a hobby, only if it's a situation that's affecting my immediate surroundings or my family. You have to sort it out, nip it in the bud. A lot of people walk down the street in fear. I hear about it when they come to my courses. Cities have changed; London has changed; Birmingham has changed and society has changed in the last thirty years. A mugging twenty years ago was a straightforward verbal affair and a snatch. Now, they'll use a weapon to get your handbag off you. It's a crazy world out there. Even if you live in a nice area, the scum will come by because of the nice cars and the nice houses. It's good pickings for them.

I've always said, 'Anyone can get into my house, but they're not going to get out.' They can come in any time they want, but that's it. What happens to them while they're in my house is between them and me. A lot of people have looked at my height and come at me because they think I'm not a problem. I'd say to anyone, 'Beware of small men and cripples.' A guy of any size can come at you in a fearsome way. But don't underestimate the small guys. People who haven't been in a boxing ring or learnt the martial arts can be very naive.

I always tell my students not to underestimate anyone. You can be the greatest athlete in the world, the hardest martial artist and do the door as a bouncer, but you can get a sixteen-year-old come up to you and put a knife in your back. You're not invincible. You've got to be alert all the time.

When I came out of the army I combined my boxing and martial-arts skills and developed several courses at my gym using both disciplines. And that's the style of fighting I teach today. I've taken four or five different methods of combat and put them together, including basic judo throws and ground/floor grappling. You need that versatility for fighting in today's society. You might end up on the floor in a confrontation, so I always train my students in floor work. When someone comes at you in the street, they're not going to fight you with association rules and a referee. You have to know what to do if someone approaches you with a knife or anything else.

Most people who come to me to train in the martial arts are more interested in acquiring these skills for self-defence rather than as a sport. I teach a cross section of styles of unarmed combat: weapons training, basic judo, grappling and boxing skills, karate and kicking techniques. People come for that knowledge. My courses take place once a week and I give an advanced one-day course every three or four months. The advanced course is mostly for those who have connections with bodyguard companies, but others hear about it and come along to improve their skills. Martial-arts skills are closely linked to close-protection work. You need those fighting skills to be a bodyguard.

I've been running courses in bodyguard and close-protection work for various institutions since about 1994. I teach the fitness and endurance techniques that are necessary to improve a bodyguard's explosive power skills. I give programmes in close protection for different situations, such as escort duties, bomb threats, checking out vehicles for drugs and explosive devices and surveillance. My knowledge in this field comes from my own experience in security work, coupled with my military experience in the Paras and the RAF Reserves. And I keep up to date with the latest techniques by going on instructors' courses.

I gained a couple of Bodyguard Instructor Diplomas a few years ago. In the awarding of these, my work in the field and my military experience were taken into account. It's what's known as Accreditation of Prior Learning and in the last few years it has been incorporated in National Vocation Qualifications and university degrees. There's little point in sending someone on a theory module if they've experienced the real thing outside of the classroom.

Once I'd decided I wanted to get into the personal-safety and self-defence business, I went along to the local college and did an Adult Education Course Teacher's Certificate. This was a theoretical course which helped me look at my own skills. It showed me how to set out a course plan and project myself better. From that, I was able to construct my own courses on personal safety.

My lessons combine theory with practice, whereas a lot of personal-safety courses are completely practical. I've introduced a classroom aspect using the whiteboard, the overhead projector and role-playing to explore different scenarios. This makes for a more informative and comprehensive programme and has been welcomed by many of the colleges at which I've taught. I think a lot of people who come along to the personal-safety lessons I give at adult-education centres expect to see someone on mats wearing a white suit and a black belt. That's not how it is. It's taken many years of experience to devise my courses, and I make the programmes and seminars casual, relaxing. I get people coming along from various career backgrounds: nurses, social workers, the unemployed, probation officers, senior management and executives.

Nurses, both male and female, often find themselves being attacked when they're on duty in a hospital. Drunks and drug addicts who are brought in are often aggressive and lash out at staff. There's an increasing need for security these days, particularly in public services. Local government officers delivering letters concerning rent arrears or social workers dealing with problems in society can feel threatened. There was a case not long ago of a planning officer being shot for delivering bad news about a house extension.

The courses on personal safety and self-defence that I run for council employees are in-depth programmes and last twelve weeks. I look at safety inside and outside the building, plus procedures to adopt when interviewing someone. Having had to go into people's houses myself when I worked for the Housing Department, I know how tense and dangerous the situation can get when there's an eviction involved. I'm able to hand on my own experiences.

I've had a number of military personnel on my courses too. My own military training has helped me to project myself and I've given a seminar for RAF wives at the Cottesmore base. These women were travelling abroad with their men and the seminar gave them that extra bit of self-awareness about living in a foreign country, plus ideas on how to watch out for the kids.

I left the RAF Regiment Reserves in May 2001, after serving two and a half years, first at Brize Norton for twelve months and then at RAF Cottesmore. I thoroughly enjoyed myself with 504 Squadron and represented them five times in various sporting events and world records, including a martial-arts kumite contest. The *RAF News* gave me a good write-up for that.

For Birmingham City Council, I also run a number of adult-education courses. A lot of people who enrol for these classes have been threatened or attacked. At the end of the course I get each person to give a ten-minute presentation, both theoretical and practical, on what they've learnt. I put them in a teaching role. I really make it hard for them and I make them think. I get them to imagine they're instructors. They're having to repeat techniques to the rest of the class and that reinforces the learning. And because of the way I deliver a course, I'm asked back again. But I always tailor the programme to the requirements of the organisation that's asked me to help.

My courses for the Adult Education Department can last for anything up to ten weeks and run every three or four months. They are held at adult-education centres, often at a college or school, and take a couple of hours in the evening. I've taught a variety of individuals on these courses, mostly people who've been threatened or mugged. They're there to regain self-esteem and self-confidence. The course gets them back on track and makes them more aware of potentially threatening situations. An evening class is a good stress-buster for some people; they want to learn how to fight.

As I found out when those four men attacked my car, you can't rely on people around you to help. That's a feature of life today: people don't want to get involved. This makes self-protection a must for individuals to learn. It's either them or us. You've got to look after yourself. But often you can only understand this once something has happened to you. Then you're more likely to say, 'OK, so Paddy's not such a headbanger or a nut case after all.' You have to understand what crime does to people who can't look after themselves. For many years afterwards they're thinking, I should have done something. They're not tortured by the memory of what happened to them; they're living with the guilt that they should have acted instead of keeping quiet.

I've had women on my courses who've been beaten up by their husbands or boyfriends. I'm happy to be a bit of a social worker and listen to their problems. There's a lot more to it than showing techniques to women who've been victimised. You've really got to build up their confidence, often on a one-to-one basis. Obviously a woman is built differently to a man, so I adapt my training and techniques to take this into account. I show women how to do the basic punches and kicks, how to use their nails to scratch eyes, how to use a handbag, an umbrella or a newspaper as a weapon. I talk about body language and how to stand and walk. Body language can project an image.

A high percentage of the women who attend my courses are sales executives. We cover, among other situations, how to look after valuables, how to deal with road rage and how to use accessories, such as keys, in self-defence. We discuss scanning techniques for checking out an area, how to avoid being stalked in a car park after leaving a business meeting or walking alone in any other place. You have to get into the habit of looking for nooks and crannies where a mugger or an attacker can hide.

If you walk down the street in a negative fashion, you're setting yourself up as a potential target. You look weak. A woman has to look up and survey the scene, take it all in. She must look positive, even if she's in area she doesn't know. Never look lost. If you don't like the look of where you are, don't hang around, get out fast. You shouldn't be there.

In my seminars for men, we likewise look at threat awareness and self-defence techniques. As with women's seminars, we focus on how to assess an aggressive situation and how to defuse it. I show them how to use voice techniques which can calm the aggressor down, rather than shouting back in the same manner.

These lessons last for five hours and are in-depth sessions, crammed with points. People walk away from them saying the course was worth attending and they've learnt a lot, that they've got real value for their money. But those who come to the seminars are mostly there as block bookings by security companies, or they're businessmen and women in suits, so I normally rent a comfortable hall rather than use my gym. My gym is a spit-and-sawdust workplace where the heating is minimal.

Once people get a bit of confidence in their instructor, they often talk about their experiences. A few years back I ran some ladies' self-defence courses and I noticed the same woman came along to the course twice. It turned out she was getting beaten up by her boyfriend. Badly beaten up. She was getting punched and kicked when he came home from the pub in the evenings. After she'd completed my first course, the boyfriend came up to her and started being aggressive towards her, as usual. She turned round and punched him in the nose. She broke it. All those years he'd been giving her grief and problems. She turned round and punched him back. You know what he did? The coward went to the police. He couldn't handle it.

Around that time I was working out in a gym in Tyseley when one day this boyfriend walks in. A mountain of a man. I didn't know him, but I could see him eyeballing me. I thought, Do I know you from another gym, or what? This happened on about three or four occasions. Every time he came to the gym, he'd be staring at me. Finally I turned round to one of the instructors in the gym and said, 'Who's that over there?'

He said, 'That's the guy whose girlfriend did your self-defence course and broke his nose.'

That's how I first heard the story. Then the girl came on another of my courses. At the end of the lesson we were having a discussion and this woman gave her story to the other ladies as an example of what they could achieve. The women didn't laugh at her. They cheered her and said, 'Fair play, dear! What a coward that man was to go to the police.' And they were right. I don't know how she did it. She was about five foot one to his six foot three. She probably used a palm strike. But it just goes to show how some men can dish it out but can't take it.

For the palm strike, you put your palm just under the tip of the aggressor's nose. You can break a nose that way. It's lethal, but it's taught in most self-defence and martial-arts courses. Even if a woman is small and weak, I can teach her to punch with power. If that fails, I've shown women how to knee or use some kicks, so they've always got something to fall back on. Never think that if your punches fail, that's it. I always give people in my classes something else they can use, so they have a combination of strike techniques and skills.

I get a lot of positive feedback from these courses. But common sense plays an important part in self-protection too. Never take short cuts when you're late for an appointment. It's worth taking the long way round in a well-lit area rather than walking down a dark alley. It's always better to be two or three minutes late for someone than to take a short cut down a narrow side-street.

I've also given personal-safety courses for elderly people. There was a lady in her sixties who came to one. I think she was a teacher or a college lecturer, a very well-to-do, professional lady. Something had happened to her when she was eighteen, and she still had nightmares about that incident all those years ago. She told me, 'Nothing serious happened to me. But I should have done something about the situation.' What had happened to her was personal, but she was disappointed she hadn't been able to do or say something at the time.

It can happen to anybody. And a self-protection course can take away that feeling of impotence. You replace it with confidence and build on it. After the way I reacted when those four men attacked my car, I've been very confident about the way I can handle myself. A few days after I'd seen off those guys, I read about a car-jacking in another part of Birmingham. A bloke had been dragged out of his nice new sports car, then they tried to run him over. The reason thieves hijack cars these days is that they can't pinch them any more. The alarm systems in cars are so hi-tech now, they've got to drag people out of their cars to thieve them.

I cover car-jacking in my courses. The main thing is never to stop your car. Keep your doors locked and stow away any valuables. If anyone approaches your car, keep your window up. These are the kind of things you should know. Use anything you can for a weapon, as long as it's legal. Carrying a knife will land you a five-year sentence.

As a rule I don't work with children, but I've helped out parents I've known whose kids were being bullied at school. Bullying can ruin a child's life. You read about them committing suicide over it these days. The kids will come along to my gym and I'll show them the fundamentals of boxing, the martial arts and fitness training to give them some confidence and improve their power. And they've gone back to school and sorted out the bully. That's good enough feedback for me.

It's a talent and a skill in itself teaching kids. What's put me off teaching them in the past was I'd be in a situation where I had to teach teenagers who were forced to learn self-defence. It's very off-putting, trying to motivate those who've given up on themselves and been expelled from school. It's hard to do, but I'm a professional and I do it. And I'm probably a bit ruthless about it, just as I was as an athlete.

Some children always say 'I can't' to everything. It starts with their home life. It may be their parents who need a good kicking. They're probably couch potatoes, sitting there smoking and drinking, who've let their kids do what they like. I believe if you've got good standards in the home, the kids will pick that up. Respect starts in your front room. Kids who've seen their parents fight will themselves end up fighting when they're adults. It's all they know. It's the only role model they have.

But there are some students I've taught who weren't motivated to start with but who've come through and shone. It was hard teaching them at first and I was biting my lip, but they did well in the end and went on to join the army or take up another interesting career. I tend to gear people towards the army because it sorted me out. I reckon I'm a good recruiter for the forces. They're more people-friendly today than when I was in. There's less shouting and bullying and they're less aggressive in training individuals. Before, you were hit and punched if you didn't do something properly, and you had to take it.

But teaching children is one-off tuition that I'll only do as a favour to someone I know. I don't often teach children, because it requires much more patience than I have. With adults, you can give them something to do and they'll do it quite happily for ten to fifteen minutes. With kids, you've got to supervise them constantly. And there are laws in place now for teaching children. Even if they go to the toilet, someone has to accompany them: there may be paedophiles out there. You've got to take all these extras on board when you're teaching children. It's all extra responsibility and it takes me away from what I really want to do.

Don't get me wrong. I love children, but instructing them is a different thing. I have friends who run martial-arts clubs and teach kids, and they're burnt out at the end of the day. You have to start from scratch and repeat exercises. I admire people for doing it, but it's hard work. Also, you have to educate a child to make sure he or she understands that his or her body is becoming a weapon and must be used responsibly. They have to be taught self-control.

But self-defence is more than learning techniques. You've got to be fit as well. You need to combine those defence skills with fitness classes, and a lot of boxing and martial-arts centres are doing this now. It's part of the learning curve. I always tell people it's not just a question of being aware and using your loaf; you must be fit.

It's mostly men who get involved in aggressive situations. A businessmen can set himself up unwittingly for a confrontation just as much as a woman can, carrying money and valuables and driving around in an executive-style car while thinking about the next business contract. The question is: should you being carrying a load of money around in one pocket, or should you split up the money into different pockets? It's not something business people think about when they're travelling from place to place.

Businesswomen often set themselves up by flashing a lot of jewellery. Anyone can forget to lock a car door and it's easy for a thief to put another chip in a stolen mobile phone. Thieves will pinch anything. You can leave a load of waste paper in a carrier bag in your car, but the thief doesn't know it's rubbish. He'll still smash the car window. It doesn't take two seconds to put your valuables in the boot or the glove compartment. The less you've got on show, the less people think of pinching things.

A few years ago some well-known people in London were getting mugged. The muggers would wait until their victims came back from their social evenings, then beat them up and take their watches and other valuables off them, and maybe their cars as well. Sometimes this would take place in a private road in a well-to-do area. The muggers would wait until the victims had got out of their car before attacking them. These criminals normally worked in gangs of two or three. They researched their targets first and carried out surveillance. It often happens that a series of crimes like this are carried out by the same gang.

A mugger, on the other hand, is often an opportunist who commits a crime on the spur of the moment. Muggers are often attracted by what I call the 'get-rich-quick syndrome' in order to buy their next fix of drugs. A lot of muggers and burglars, up to the age of about eighteen, are short of money for a drink or drugs. And a lot more of them are carrying weapons now.

I did an on-the-spot survey at my gym the other day while I was teaching. Every member of my gym drives a car. I asked them, 'Which of you carries a weapon in the car?' All the hands went up. Even taxi drivers carry weapons. It's against the law, but everyone's got a hammer and all sorts with them, even people driving nice cars. It could be they've forgotten to take their DIY stuff out of the car, but it could be down to crime or the road-rage factor.

If someone came at you with a knife, I'd advise you to do a bit of monkey kung fu: grab the nearest thing to you, on the floor or beside you. It can be coins in your pocket or a brick or a stone or some sand. You use this to create a distance between you and the aggressor. Anyone can do this, even if they're not trained in self-defence. Coins can be thrown at the face, and if there's a brick on the ground, pick it up and aim it where you see fit.

If there's an intruder in your home, you need to defend yourself. If I came downstairs and found a burglar in my house, I'd restrain him. That's a good response to put in front of a magistrate. If the intruder has a bump on his head or he collected any bruises before the police arrived, he'd have got them when he landed on the floor while you were restraining him and accidentally landed on top of him.

The International Bodyguard Union, the IBU, is an organisation I've been involved with since about 1998. It was set up by Richard Hopkins, the president of WUMA. Richard is a former bodyguard and doorman, as well as a top martial artist, and has a large number of staff around him to run his organisation. The IBU was set up to give courses on close protection and security for those who want to go into bodyguard work, and the organisation maintains a register of qualified and graded bodyguards for close-protection work.

Good training is vital in security work. A senior doorman, who's an acquaintance of mine and now an instructor, tells of an incident which happened in a nightclub in London in the mid-nineties. The doormen in the club spotted a drug dealer going about his work and they decided to get him out of the place. They went over and escorted him out. But they were looking at the drug dealer as they accompanied him to the door. They didn't realise or think that the man had his pals, his runners, doing some selling for him in the club. The runners closed in to protect the drug dealer and two of the doormen got knifed. One was killed.

It was lack of training. A lack of teamwork. The doormen should not have been looking at the drug dealer. They should have been looking around, scanning the outer circle. But, by focusing on the drug dealer and thinking how good they felt about getting the guy out, they came a cropper. Training is so important. If they'd been doing their job properly, the doormen would have searched the people going in for knives and other weapons. Security starts on the front door. That confrontation should have been at the door, not in the club. But it was too late.

I still do a small amount of top-level protection work myself. But it's not a regular thing for me these days. I'll always look at a special assignment and, if I can fit it in, including the travel, I'll go for it. My reasoning is, if you're prepared to pay good money, you'll get the best protection money can buy. Pay peanuts and you'll get monkeys.

Earlier this year I was asked to teach at a bodyguard school in South Africa, but I had to turn it down because of other commitments. They said to me, 'Make sure you're armed when you get off the plane, Paddy.' That's the level of threat they're facing out there. It's a bad place for muggings and shootings. Being armed doesn't bother me at all. I'm used to handling weapons and I wouldn't hesitate to use one if I had to. I kept up my skills in the RAF, training at weekends on assault courses, rifle-range practice and other soldiering. I'm not the world's greatest shot but I'm good with a bayonet. It releases a lot of aggression in me. I did more bayonet training in the Paras than in the Reserves, and I'm happier with hand-to-hand combat.

I may do some more soldiering in the Reserves in the future. They know I don't have to do the training because I've already got the experience. Ex-Regular Reserves are sometimes asked to come on board to join the Regulars. The army wants all the experience it can get. And I'd love to take up that challenge again. I miss the comradeship. It's got to be better than sitting at home watching TV.

I'm also a part-time bodyguard instructor for Clearwater Associates Close Protection, a security services company set up by Kevin Horak and based in Shrewsbury. They're a very professional group: top-level instructors from the military and the police, and they're recognised by various vocational institutions and have contacts with the Home Office. An associate of Clearwater is Tecar, managed by Terry Caroll, a former captain in the Red Devils. He looks after surveillance. I respect these people and enjoy working with them all.

We got together when they heard good things about my courses in self-defence, personal safety and unarmed combat. They asked me to devise a course for men and women who wanted to become bodyguards. Some of these people had done self-defence before and some hadn't. They're assessed and examined in practice and theory throughout the course by the IBU. The courses are called 'Fight to Survive' and they take place every three or four months.

Clearwater Associates maintain a register of bodyguards they've trained and they recommend them for close-protection work with large companies and corporations who approach them. They provide surveillance teams and run investigations, both corporate and private. If a company needed to investigate an internal problem – for example, a run of thefts, or there was a suspicion of industrial spying within a corporation – Clearwater could plant someone on the inside to see what was going down. I know a few people who are working as plants in London firms at the moment. But you never discuss names or companies. Those people on the inside are putting their lives at risk, and those of their families, just being there. It's a very close-knit network, very hush-hush.

It's about how well you can deliver the goods on courses, whether it's physical fitness and endurance, explosive power techniques or unarmed-combat training. My bodyguard courses for private firms are more intensive than the adult-education courses I give in self-protection. The bodyguard training stretches over a seven-day period but each day is packed with about eight or nine hours of training. With Clearwater, I've taken on the unarmed combat and self-defence side of bodyguard work. With the IBU, I focus on fitness and endurance and explosive power skills.

To teach someone to realise explosive power, I give them a combination of exercises. These involve punching skills and circuit training, such as press-ups and sit-ups, and I combine these with self-defence techniques. When I give trainees punching and kicking skills, I show them when to use them. The kind of technique that's useful to know is how to make one pure strike, instead of a lot of strikes during which you can get grabbed by the opposition. One effective strike can be enough to immobilise an aggressor.

I get a lot of excellent feedback from my courses. Individuals who've done unarmed combat and self-defence training before and who are instructors in their own field have come back to me and said, 'That's something new I've learnt.' They're involved in the same field of work as me, and at the same level, but they've learnt new skills, even if it's only one move or technique, and thanked me for it. I've helped them protect their own clients or pass on knowledge to their students in their club. As in any career, knowledge is an ongoing thing in my field. Everyone's exchanging ideas with everyone else. It's about networking.

Although I'm still young enough for the bodyguard world and can do the job hands-on, my knowledge and experience make me more useful to companies as an instructor. Most people can continue as a bodyguard into their mid-forties without a problem. It's down to health and fitness. As a bodyguard, you might get a client who likes running every morning. The point is, you've got to be prepared for anything and be able to adapt fast. The money's good in this line of work, especially if you get a client from abroad.

By the time you're forty-five, you'll probably want to start teaching and hand on your experience anyway. I'm not saying it's downhill after forty-five, but you'd normally want to get into the management side of the business; you'd want to run teams. It would be the right moment because you're comparatively young and you have the mental and physical energy to run courses.

A lot of international clients rate British security training very highly. Many global companies prefer British agencies to do their bodyguard work for them. Oil companies and the larger information technology companies, who have outposts in countries where extortion, corruption and kidnapping are common, ask for protection from UK ex-military bodyguards. Our SAS and Paras have a reputation abroad for being highly trained. A lot of foreign armies model themselves on the British forces, and many international companies ask former British military personnel to train their own security staff.

But there are a lot of jobs we don't talk about. Not ever. There's a code in the close-protection business. And we all depend on each other to stick to that code.

CHAPTER 10

EXPLOSIVE POWER

CLOSE-PROTECTION WORK isn't like the other sports disciplines I focus on. It's employment. I get paid for giving courses and protecting people. But there's no way you can do this kind of work without being fit. You have to be able to fight and defend yourself. You need a high level of awareness, stamina and experience.

I was teaching fighting skills before I went on my first self-defence coaching course in 1993. I was only accepted on that course because I was a martial-arts teacher. At that time I could see that colleges weren't running any personal-safety courses. I approached one or two of them and proposed some programmes, then set up my self-protection courses for women. The programmes were immediately popular. I was known in the area for being a competitive athlete and that made me a bit more interesting than the average instructor. I had an extra layer of knowledge and experience.

All sorts of people began registering for the courses, from those who'd learnt self-defence before to those who hadn't. I still get a range of students today. Even those who've already done some sort of martial-arts training feel it's good to go on a course to refresh themselves. I encourage that. It's possible to forget skills. And, if people want to work as a bodyguard or a doorman, I'll pass them on to Clearwater Associates, who specialise in close-protection services of all types.

Most of the people who come to me because they're interested in bodyguard work are already working in the close-protection field. They're normally on one of my courses to learn more techniques for looking after their clientele. These are very thorough courses. So much knowledge is thrown at people in seven days, for eight or nine hours a day, it's unbelievable. They learn about everything from surveillance to dealing with the media on behalf of a client. They learn how to check a vehicle for bombs, escort clients to vehicles, unarmed combat, weapons awareness, self-defence and fitness training.

I don't advertise. I get my students by word of mouth. And I don't enter anyone for competitions because usually we don't have the time. I use my classes to motivate people to learn new skills and students come regularly for WUMA gradings and belts. WUMA is tough enough, but I throw in a few extras to make it tougher. I'll demonstrate an exercise to my students, then get them to do it.

We do a lot of stamina workouts because I've always said you've got to be fit to fight. You need a strong neck and strong abdominal muscles. Ultimately it's about stamina and explosive power. You have to be able to last not two minutes but ten minutes, if need be. Fitness and stamina mean your body is stronger and therefore more able to withstand punishment, take the knocks. If you're not strong and you get kicked or punched, you're not going to survive.

A lot of women who come on my courses have stopped making excuses for the way their men behave towards them. They'll stand up and say, 'This has happened to me.' And their next sentence is: 'But it's not going to happen any more.' That's when I know I've achieved something as an instructor. These women aren't going to be shoved around any more.

And older men and women, pensioners who get pushed around, should be taught how to defend themselves; how to punch, kick and elbow their way out of a situation. Sometimes, when I've given a course for local government, I've invited the police along to cover the law on how far you can defend yourself. They'll take half an hour to run through the basic points. It's important to get the right agencies to cover special areas. My friend Wayne Bernstein, from the West Midlands Police, came along and gave a talk during one of my personal-safety courses for social workers.

I show people on my courses not only how to punch and kick, but how also to restrain someone by the shoulder or the arm. At the same time it's important that anyone involved in

close-protection work understands how far they can go before
their defence is interpreted as an attack. You have to know your
own strength and when to stop. Otherwise the attacker can
become the victim. Then it's up to the individual to explain the
situation to the magistrate.

There are a lot of bodybuilders out there, big, strong guys who
reckon they're tough. They train in the gym to be good punchers
and kickers and fighters. They train their bodies but they don't
train their minds in how to deal with being interviewed by the
police should they get arrested for dealing with a confrontation.
If you're going to restrain somebody, it's best done in twos rather
than by one person. If you're on your own and you get arrested,
make it clear to officers that you thought your life was in danger,
you thought you were about to die, that you were only defending
yourself to the best of your ability.

When you're walking down the street, experience will tell you
if there's trouble brewing. Experience is a strength in itself. If
there's a gang hanging around on a street corner, they could be
looking for a weak target. You have to know how to handle that,
how to walk positively down the road. It's how you carry yourself,
body language, how you project yourself. I teach people how to
appear positive, how to hold their head up high.

If you look at people walking along, you'll often see someone
looking at the ground, looking negative and miserable. They can't
see where an aggressor is going to spring from; they can't scan
areas. Appearances count and so does projecting a strong
personality. And that comes from the mind.

The increase in drugs on the streets means that you can be attacked by someone who has no fear. That's what drugs do: they alter the mind of a person. He has no inhibitions. A high percentage of muggings these days are down to drugs. The junkie has to mug someone for money for his next fix. He may be an eight-stone weakling, but his drug will make him feel like a twenty-stone strong man.

Alcohol mixed with drugs is another heavy cocktail. I recently went on a course for tutors on how to teach drugs awareness. You learn what drugs can do to people, and you need to know that in the security business. People sometimes take drugs to give them the balls to commit a crime. You need to be aware of the kind of behaviour you might be confronted with. And, if you're a doorman working in a club, you have to be aware of the effects of ecstasy. This drug keeps people going but they can become aggressive.

A decade ago there wasn't the training for doormen that there is now. Nowadays a training course is often a step up for a doorman and he'll become a bodyguard or he'll manage a team of doormen because of his extra knowledge. The government runs courses now for health and safety and drugs awareness, and you can't become a doorman if you've got a criminal record. The whole scene has improved.

A few years ago standards on the door weren't always the best and possibly created friction. Now it's all about customer care and selling the club image. 'Good evening. How are you?' is what you'll hear. Doormen are also taught how to search for knives, and there are scanners for detecting weapons that an individual might be carrying.

The British government is now using private security firms in the courts and to run prisons. More and more governments around the world are looking to private companies for their security contracts. There are private security firms working in hospitals, airports and in other public organisations. But someone who wants to work in security still has to go through a vetting procedure. It's necessary to make sure he or she is the right person for the job.

Close-protection work can last for half an hour or a week, or longer. It can be an escort job or you may have to check out someone's house. If there are any easy entrances to the property, you advise the client to get them sorted out. You look at the boundaries, the fences. You make sure they have a safe for their valuables. It may sound simple, but people often forget the simple things. They think once they're home, they're safe inside the four walls. But that's not always the case.

When you drive a client somewhere, you have to be looking around at the same time. When you pull up, you get out of the car first and scan the location, and continue looking around you while the client leaves the vehicle.

Surveillance work is normally commissioned by insurance companies, and often happens when someone is suspected of making a false claim. Airport security, especially after the attack on the World Trade Center, depends on staff training and the knowledge of the instructor. An instructor with military experience is always a bonus because ex-military personnel look at situations from a wider perspective.

Apart from in London, there isn't a great deal of close-protection work in the UK. Most people in the security business end up working abroad. Princess Diana's bodyguard was ex-military. I know two ex-Royal Marine Commandos who work overseas, and one ex-Special Forces person who works for an oil company as a consultant and hires ex-military personnel to work with him abroad. If you're lucky enough to get on the celebrity circuit in London, you're fine; otherwise you have to go overseas.

A bodyguard must be disciplined; he must be able to think on his feet and solve problems as they arise. He must be adaptable. He may be on duty all night and have to continue working into the next day. A lot of clients are abrupt in their manner and you have to be able to bite your tongue. The client's not going to worry about his manners because he's paying you, and you put up with that because the money's good.

Ideally, a bodyguard will have military experience. That means he or she is trained to respond quickly, in any situation, and can handle the pressure that comes with it. It also means you know how to work in a team and manage a team. Martial-arts skills are important too. Boxing, judo and other fighting techniques are a distinct advantage. You never know when you're going to need those skills.

One evening I was having a quiet drink with Desi Clifton and another mate in a club in Birmingham. Our friend happened to run a pub, and while we were drinking he received a telephone call from his wife to say a number of gypsies had gone in there and were refusing to leave.

The three of us went along to his pub to see what was going down. We found the gypsies were still there, even though it was after closing time. They were adamant they wouldn't leave until they'd been served some more drink. We told them it was time to go. At that point one of the gypsies came at me, nose to nose. It was obvious he was going to hit me, so I struck him first, under the jaw.

The guy went straight up in the air, so I'm told. I wasn't aware of it. I was on a different planet; somewhere else. He landed on a table and, even though it was one of those pub tables with wrought-iron legs, the whole thing collapsed underneath him. Another gypsy came at me. I hit him on the jaw and put him down. By now I was well into my work. I probably needed help in cooling down. My friend, the guy who owned the pub, put his arms around the back of me to restrain me. He brought me down but, because he was still behind me, I couldn't see him. I thought he was another gypsy. I threw my head back and cracked his cheekbone. He collapsed on the floor.

I went outside, leaving Desi in the pub watching the situation. He'd been making sure no one put a table or a chair on my head from behind. But another gypsy was right behind me, following me to the corner of the street. The guy came right at me, I swear.

So I hit him; I put him down. Somebody was shouting, 'Get the police!' By that time I knew I had to get out of it fast.

I heard the police siren wailing. I ran across the road and jumped into some bushes. The bushes were right beside a big billboard and I waited there for Desi to come out and collect me, so we could do a runner. The police arrived and went into the pub. They wanted to know what had been going on. One of the gypsies pointed at Desi and said he was with me. Desi, quick off the mark as ever, said, 'No, mate. You've got it wrong. I'm the taxi driver.' The police left, after the owners of the pub had explained how it had all happened, and the place calmed down.

Meanwhile I'm stuck, fifteen foot up in the air, having climbed up the struts at the back of the hoarding, thinking the police were coming for me. I saw Desi come out of the pub and I popped my head over the billboard and shouted down to him, 'Meet you round the back!' I climbed down and went round to the rear of the pub, so the police wouldn't see me if they were waiting anywhere to arrest me. We hopped in Desi's car and he drove me home. As Desi said, seeing me stuck at the top of the hoarding, it was a nice finishing touch to a bar-room brawl.

Next morning I went back to my friend's pub. I rang the bell and stood outside and waited. After a while a patched-up face appeared at the bedroom window. I could see the guy was in a bad way. 'Oi, mate!' I yelled up to him. 'Are you going to sponsor me for my next world record then?'

There was a pause. Then he said, 'How much do you want?'

'Four hundred and fifty pounds!' I shouted back.

A cheque floated down from the bedroom window and I caught it in my hands. I like to think it was a 'thank you' note for a bit of door work the night before.

A lot of my confrontations have been about defending myself when I've been threatened or I've been trying to help others. The moment someone threatens me, they cross the line. It's happened many times. One night in the late eighties, I was out with a friend who's a police officer and we decided to go along to a pub in Birmingham. The guy on the door said, 'Nobody's coming in!' and he pushed me backwards. He wouldn't let me in.

I said, 'Why are you pushing me? We only want a quiet drink.' I couldn't understand why he was being aggressive towards me. There was no reason for it. He was bigger than me and he was standing on a step. Well, I punched him and he flew backwards. My friend and I got out of there fast. Just after that I met someone who told me the guy I'd punched was the landlord of the pub. But I also heard the bloke was arrogant. And he must have been in a bad mood. But he shouldn't have struck me on the chest. You don't push potential customers about.

A few years later I went for a drink with a solicitor who'd just defended me in court after a spot of bother. I got fined by the court and the solicitor suggested we go for a drink afterwards. We went along to a private bar where all the magistrates and lawyers go after being in court, and who should be in the bar? The guy I'd struck on the step, the landlord. It turned out the bloke was a friend of the solicitor I was with.

He said, 'You don't remember me, do you?' I didn't recognise him. 'You bust my nose.' Then I knew who he was. He went on, 'But I deserved it.' We shook hands, and that was it. We parted on good terms. Just goes to show how your past can catch up with you.

The reason I'd been in court that day was I'd gone a bit wild on the town one night. I was at a club with my two cousins when three Scottish guys started causing us trouble. They'd had a few shandies and I'd had a few shandies myself. We told them we'd see them outside. My cousins came outside with me to watch my back. One of the Scots went for me. I hit him and put him on the floor, knocked him out. The next one came at me. I knocked him out. The third one jumped on my back and I threw him over me. Then I got arrested. The police had been patrolling the area.

In court, the three Scots stood up. The magistrate said to them, 'Tell me what happened.'

One of them said, 'Well, your honour, Mr Doyle hit me. He hit my friend, and he hit my other friend.'

The magistrate turned to me, looking at the size of me. Everyone in the court started to titter. The whole thing sounded pretty comic. I ended up getting a small fine.

When I'd been arrested, I was taken along to Steel House Lane police station, then released after they'd taken my details. I hadn't been so lucky on other occasions. I'd had a confrontation with the plate-glass window of an Indian restaurant one evening. I'd been experimenting with the plastic ventilator in the glass and the whole thing came out in my hands, including the rest of the window. It was like the time I took the putty out of my neighbour's porch windows when I was a kid. Only I'd had a few drinks this time and I was in real trouble.

The point was, I wasn't in the restaurant when this happened. I was outside on the pavement, and the glass was all around me. I went off to find a taxi and someone called the police. They stopped the taxi and hauled me off to Steel House Lane police station, which is like a big holding place, and I was fined for that mishap too.

Another time I was in a curry house and I got into an argument about some money I felt I was owed. I must have done a runner because the police came round that night and took me off to the Steel House Lane station again. I'd been told I was only going there for a quick interview, but I got locked up for the fucking weekend over a fiver. And when I got to court, the waiter in the restaurant couldn't recognise me. So that was the end of that.

People often ask me how they should sort out a problem, and I'm always happy to advise them. But I'll only give advice; I won't sort out the problem myself, like I did in the past. I've had enough of all that. These days I'm only interested in looking after my own property.

A few years back a neighbour of mine was acting strangely. I think he had a problem with drink and drugs. We had a dispute over something and the guy came over, kicked my front door and left a footmark. I went across to his house and kicked his door in. And when I saw him at the bottom of the stairs, I hit him. I didn't strike him hard, but I underestimated my strength and he fell on the floor. I thought he would have put up a better fight than he did. I said, 'Don't do that again. Don't touch my property.'

Next thing I know, the guy calls the police and I'm cautioned. I explained to the officers it was a domestic situation and I was dealing with the problem as it arose. OK, I had threatened to kill him, but if I'd come across to the guy as weak and negative, the situation might have continued. It was the school bully syndrome all over again.

I only teach people on my courses how to defend themselves if they're getting pushed about. One of the points of a course is to give a person confidence. Giving them an idea what to do if their back is against the wall.

One time I was in Ireland, giving a security course for a group of military personnel, and I had a few pints with some of the lads at the end of the class. One of them told me his aunt was getting beaten up by someone who, if my memory serves me correctly, belonged to an organisation that wasn't averse to violence itself. He was a nice bloke, lovely chap, and he wanted to go round and sort out the situation. I said I'd help him.

I managed to find a balaclava and a big lump of wood, ready to take this other guy out. We had it all planned. I'd told my friend how we were going to do it. We'd give the guy a good hiding, that was all. We arranged to meet up at five o'clock in the morning, but he didn't turn up. Later he told me he'd decided to sort out the situation himself, in his own way. He said he didn't want to get me involved. Just as well really. He might have got his kneecaps blown off after I'd left for England.

* * *

Close-protection work is becoming competitive in this country. It's important that employees are kept up to date with situations and techniques to deal with them. Crime is like fashion: it changes. One minute it's credit-card swindling or nicely dressed people, bent on theft, talking their way into an office; the next minute it's something more violent. You try to be one step ahead of what's going on.

Basic skills, such as the martial arts, will always be relevant but you have to update yourself and others on the latest fashion in criminal thinking. I keep up with a lot of people from my past. I may be one side of the fence these days, but I still have memories of being on the other. I'll have a drink now and again with people who are my friends, but I don't get involved in anything I shouldn't. I understand I'm a role model for some of the young lads and I've got an image to maintain.

But friends from the past are still friends. What they do to make a living is their business. We have a drink and a laugh. It's not for me to tell them what they can and can't do. They don't tell me what they're doing and I don't ask. That doesn't bother me. I've always been a character and I'll always have characters around me.

The best marketplace for a bodyguard these days is the corporate business area. For that kind of job you have to be well dressed, and smart. Sometimes corporate management themselves are threatened. I've been approached by businessmen who've needed looking after for short periods of time. I've escorted them to the bank when they've been carrying money or important documents, and I've made sure they've got to evening venues safely. When you're walking with someone, you're looking about you the whole time but you're blending in with the background. You don't want to stand out. Everyone's idea of a bodyguard is someone who's six foot six, muscle-bound and wearing dark glasses. It's not the case. Nine times out of ten it's somebody five foot eight or nine who's dressed to merge with the surroundings. You've got to be shrewd about it.

Before escorting a client, you do your research. You find out as much as you can about the client and you check out the premises involved to see where a threat might come from. I never take a job without knowing who I'm looking after; it gives me a better idea of the kind of enemy or attacker he's trying to avoid. I look at the kind of vehicle he's driving. You don't want to be travelling in a car that might break down. And if it's a regular run, you make sure you vary the route and the times.

When I get to the venue, I'm looking at emergency exits and people that don't fit into the crowd in some way. I try to get a list of names of those who might be a threat to my client, along with a description of them. And I try to have a comprehensive talk with the client about why he thinks he's in danger and from whom. Never take a situation at face value. Do your groundwork. It's professional. Once you've done that, it makes the job a lot easier and the situation is less threatening for you, as well.

One or two bodyguards, through lack of experience, might say 'Yes' to a job and turn up at the appointed time. A lot of blokes standing in the dole queue will take on work like that for fifty quid. They don't know what they're looking for or who they're driving for, and if they get a good hiding on the job, it's justified. Someone may have a grudge against a businessman because he hasn't been paid. That's the kind of work that often comes in.

The technical side of security is an expensive game. I've been shown how to use bugs and other equipment but you can't be an expert in everything. I've channelled my skills in another direction and I'm an expert in my own field. The technological side of security isn't as interesting for me as the nitty-gritty combat training and showing people how to prepare themselves for knocks and bumps. I'm more a front-of-stage bloke than behind the scenes.

Sometimes I get businessmen who are emotional about the threats they've received and I do my best to calm them down. A while back a restaurant owner came to my gym. He was getting problems from other people in his line of business and receiving threats. He was very upset. He wanted to purchase a gun with a silencer. I don't know where he got the idea that I sold guns. I don't sell or buy and I don't give out either. I said, 'I can't get you a gun but I can teach you self-defence and help you get your act together.'

I calmed him down and supplied him with some ex-military contacts in security to look after his restaurant and escort him to the bank. Something must have worked because he didn't get back to me. Ex-military guys like myself recommend one another when someone calls on us for expert help.

I'm the self-defence instructor for the World Association of Special Forces, which is only open to ex-Special Forces personnel. The WASF runs a number of courses which help to keep your skills sharp, such as hostage-avoidance, street-patrolling, bodyguard and survival courses.

The programmes are very advanced; we did the basic training when we were in the military. During a hostage-avoidance course I went on recently they set up a killing house. You had to get in there and take out the hostage. The guys with me were mostly on the military reserve list but some were ex-Special Forces and now in the protection business. They were made up of ex-Foreign Legion, ex-Belgian Paratroopers, British Paras and Territorial Army. Most of them are on the military reserve list. We were doing fourteen-hour days on that course and it wasn't without incident. We weren't using live ammunition, just high-powered pellets, and we were all masked up so we couldn't get injured. But I accidentally shot a guy in the mouth. One of my pellets pierced his lip. He was all right, thank God.

You end up with a few injuries to your back and your knees on the assault courses the WASF puts you through. They're very thorough and do everything in depth. It's a refresher programme but it's hard and challenging, even though we've done it all before. We're not a mercenary group: we're there to support our forces, if we're called up. We're a body of international ex-servicemen of a very high calibre. We've helped out in an advisory capacity with security overseas, where the threat of kidnapping and hostage taking is very real for private global companies. There are several companies in the UK who are recognised at government level for their global security services and I've trained some of their military personnel myself.

The WASF also raises money for the benevolent funds of various regiments. It's a good association to belong to and I'm glad to be an active unit member.

You're not allowed to use a gun in the UK and most of Europe, but you can do so, if the weapon is registered, in certain countries on other continents. The type of gun you'd use would depend on the job. If the client is travelling, you have to do your research and find out if the country he's going to is classed as high-risk. Check with the Home Office, or even the local travel agent: what's the political situation like? Are kidnappings frequent there? Are shootings regular occurrences? Do you need to wear a bulletproof vest? You have to watch the back of people as well as the front.

Women who do close-protection work are called female operatives to distinguish them from the men. I've taught women on my last few courses on close-protection work and there's actually a shortage of women in the field. Some clients require women to do a job. They blend into the background nicely. No one is looking for a woman.

Bodyguards don't have any more power than anyone else. They can make a citizen's arrest, but anyone can do that. They have to keep up their training, though. On courses, we give people tips on how to maintain their fitness. Going for a run is a simple way of keeping fit. And you can find out where the local gym is for when you have time off. You can also do circuit training in your own room: press-ups, sit-ups and squat thrusts. All of these keep up your stamina level. Physical fitness gives you an altogether different level of confidence. If you feel fit, you feel good about yourself. And that's good for strength of mind. An unfit bodyguard isn't going to be able to face a threatening situation; he won't feel confident about himself.

I've seen someone fall apart on a job: a doorman I knew at a restaurant. He was a black belt in karate. I'd been in the ring with the guy a few times at my gym, sparring with him for some competition he was going in for. He was also training to join a karate squad who were going abroad to fight. A drunkard, a big guy, who'd already been banned from the restaurant, came along and started causing trouble. I went to help the doorman out and this big drunkard turned on me.

I was standing on a step but the guy was still taller than me. I turned round and gave him a left hook. I had to, as I knew he was going to come for me. The bloke fell like a ton of bricks. I said goodnight to my friend and got in my car and drove off. Unfortunately the doorman lost his job after that. The management wasn't sure he could handle it. But he was a nice lad and he still laughs about the way I sorted the other fellow out.

When I'm teaching unarmed combat training at my gym, people sometimes come along from other clubs to improve their techniques. Occasionally, when I'm sparring with them in the ring, they'll try to take advantage of me. I say to my regulars, 'If you're going to hit hard, expect to be hit hard back.' One guy I'd been saying that to for a whole month was taking no notice. I finally put my foot down and he had to go to the dentist the next morning. I think his jaw and teeth had been pushed back slightly. I heard a crunch when I hit him. It must have been a good central punch to get the jaw, nose and teeth at the same time. We continued the sparring session, but the guy had learnt the very hard way. He was down on one knee in the corner of the ring. But I always say, 'If you hit out at your senior instructor, then someone's going to have to put some manners on you.'

Sparring is about practising your fighting skills, but in my gym I get a lot of people who've fought before; they've done Thai boxing and karate. They would really like to have a battle and get my name under their belt. I have to expect that and be ready for it. As senior instructor, I get them coming at me, but I try to give them plenty of warning before I fight back. It's not professional to knock people out in your own club. But if they're deaf, you've got to clear their ears.

Another time a lad who was a doorman came to the gym. He'd boxed before and won a martial-arts title. He joined the club and trained with me for a long time. I was carrying an injury after a street confrontation and this guy was aware of that. I wasn't one hundred per cent fit. He was coming at me, punching me as hard as he could. I couldn't do anything about it; I was just getting back into training after my injury. The following week I really knocked him all over the place and got him in the corner and pummelled him. I gave him a good lesson in head and body punches.

About a month after that another guy came to the club. Big lad. I found out he was part of some top karate squad. He'd represented the UK on a couple of occasions. He told me he'd never boxed or punched before. I told him I do both, the martial arts and boxing, and that we'd have a nice, steady couple of rounds. He came out firing big right-hand punches at me. I thought, Right. First round, I matched him. Second round, I gave him a real dig. His head was like a punchball on a spring, going backwards and forwards. That was enough for him.

In any martial-arts class, you're shown how to punch. They don't just show you how to use your feet and kick. If a martial artist says to me he doesn't know how to punch, he's normally saying that out of fear; he doesn't know what my strength is going to be. He'll say something like that so he can get a punch in first, as hard as he can.

More recently a guy who'd done some full-contact martial arts and won a silver medal at a London venue came to my gym. He was good with his feet. He could kick. He was part of a squad training session when I was getting ready for a world-record attempt. I said to him, 'Look at the way I spar with the other lads, nice and simple. It's contact, but it's controlled.' He saw this, so he knew how he should fight me. Instead he came at me and kicked me in the groin, but I had a box on to protect myself. Then he kicked me around the head and gave me a forward kick in the stomach. I thought that, being a qualified martial artist and a black belt with competition experience, he'd have more sense. Second round, I boxed him all over the place and used my kicks. I gave him a grazed eye and put him out of the ring. He fell through the ropes.

I often get challenged, but it's much harder when it happens in my club. These are men who are sober, qualified and experienced. They know what they're doing. They know how to hurt. That's a proper challenge. It's far harder than having a punch-up in a bar for a few seconds over a drink. In the gym, you're up against an expert, not some legless goon with a big mouth and Dutch courage.

Every boxing, kumite or martial-arts challenge I've achieved has been with my bare hands, not guns or knives. I've never used weapons. I've always used my bare knuckles, or my feet or my head in a confrontation. I haven't looked for fights. Some people either go out looking for trouble or they set themselves up for it. But when trouble comes my way, I deal with it there and then. I'll assess the threat and sort it out as fast as I can and to the best of my ability. It's fight and flight. That's my advice to anyone in a confrontation: get out of the situation as soon as possible. If you're being attacked or the odds are against you, don't stand around and try to be a hero; do what you've got to do and disappear.

If you work in the close-protection field, keep training and updating your skills. Don't do one course and think, That's enough for me. Have an open mind and keep learning, because new kinds of security threats are coming along all the time. It's one of the reasons the martial arts have changed their techniques over the years: they have to deal with new situations. Security training programmes are regularly revised because the nature of the work keeps shifting. We live in a changing world and we have to adapt.

CHAPTER 11

FITNESS AND ENDURANCE

IT'S HARD TO DEFINE the term 'endurance'. To me it describes an event that takes place over a long period of time. And, believe me, one to three hours when you're going for a record is a long time. As well as my skills in boxing and the martial arts, I'm an endurance athlete with mountain and hill backpack records. I'm also a gymnastic and circuit-training athlete with world records for press-ups and squat thrusts.

Fitness is different from endurance, and speed is different again from endurance. For fitness and endurance athletes, an hour's event would be a speed event, whereas for a regular athlete a ten-minute event where he covers fifteen hundred metres could be a speed event. Anything above an hour for a fitness athlete would become an endurance event.

I started my first fitness club at the Magnet Centre, Park

Approach, in Erdington, in the late eighties. The Centre closed in 1993 and I've had my present gym for about ten years now. It's a part-time club. I rented the first gym when I started to get into the instructor side of sport. I wanted to pass on my skills and have a club as a centre of excellence. I wanted people to come to me to learn new techniques and to improve their fitness and stamina for their particular sport, whether it was the martial arts or boxing.

To find new premises, I made enquiries and drove around; people were getting to know my name and were happy to help out. I found a squash court at the Holly Lane Sports and Social Centre in Erdington and set about converting it into a gym. The venue is used for a variety of sports, including football, cricket and badminton. I put in a boxing ring and punchbags, gloves and martial-arts equipment and called it Staminas Boxing Self Defence Centre. It's a pre-war, spit-and-sawdust place. Dull-looking green paint everywhere. There's nothing flash about it.

It's a cold and eerie place when you first walk in. Dead quiet. Like walking into a dungeon. One of the lads at the gym likened it to walking into hell, because of the standards of training we set: aggressive, no-nonsense teaching. It's a place of preparation where you reach a good, all-round fighting standard, but it's a rough-and-ready place. When it rains, the roof leaks. I remember, one time, half the gym was flooded; there was half an inch of water on the floor. But I still made everyone work out and do sit-ups and press-ups in the wet. I've done it myself, carried on training throughout the flooding and mopped up afterwards.

The gym became the base for training and preparation for my

record attempts. It was like an HQ; it was where the team gathered. We rehearsed the record attempts with stopwatches. It was sweat and adrenalin, shouting and swearing. We dug in and worked hard. I still use the place for coaching and martial-arts gradings, bodyguard and doormen courses and self-defence lessons for men and women.

I also visit the homes of business people and coach them on a one-to-one basis. These clients are normally successful people in their forties and I quite enjoy the work. But I've been doing it all for a long time now and I'm thinking about taking a break from everything and going walking. A change is as good as a rest.

From the age of eight until I retired from record breaking at the end of 2001, I'd been involved in competitive sport, against other people or the clock. In 2001 I thought, It's time to take a break before I burn out. But, after a couple of months without a goal, I'm bored to tears. I decided to get my house sorted out, but I'm definitely at a sort of crossroads in my life. I've always been a winner; I've always been positive in whatever I approach, so I'll make sure nothing around me fails to take off. But I wouldn't want to run a gym full time. I'd feel desk-bound. I'm happier out in the field, meeting people. I'm one for moving around, doing courses in Wales or up north. Out and about, that's me.

I remember doing one of the multi-terrain courses in Leek, Staffordshire. It was the Cloud 7 Circuit for the twenty-eight-mile Multi Terrain Challenge. It took place on one of the hottest days of the year and I had to do the course wearing a forty-pound backpack. That was tough. The hills were very steep inclines. I was in a team of six or seven but it was catching out the lads, one by one, and they were dropping out with heat exhaustion. That meant I was losing my pacers as I was going round, so I had to rest and wait for them to join me again later. But the heat really knocked everyone back. It affected the whole team.

Because of my gym work, I meet a large number of very fit people. Endurance sport does that; it improves stamina and performance. But, looking around, I think sporting standards in schools are not as high as they used to be and there's less encouragement for kids to take up sports. As an instructor, I think the ages of eight or nine are the golden years for learning. The children are still flexible in their bodies but they're old enough to learn. You don't forget the things you learn before the age of ten. Break falls and other holds you learn when you're young tend to spring to mind when you're tested later on, or if you go back into the sport.

At the same time people who do train are a lot fitter than they were ten or fifteen years ago. More is known about how to keep your body on top form and there are new techniques and programmes for training. There are therapists who specialise in sports injuries and I rate them highly for their treatments. You still have to rest an injury but a sports therapist can speed up recovery. They'll massage a damaged joint and give you advice on nutrition to help the healing process.

I'm not a nutritionist, but I take one or two supplements because I believe they help me personally. I take ginseng and guarana to help repair damaged muscles, but neither is cheap.

Every morning I take these and a multivitamin pill and a capsule of cod-liver oil. I've been swallowing cod-liver oil every day for the last sixteen years and I rate it very highly. You have to watch what you eat when you're training for a record. You can't afford to be ill. Eat the wrong takeaway meal and you're up all night sick. You're dehydrated and your training schedule is affected.

But I don't hold with crank diets. Everything in moderation: a little food but often to keep your energy level up. A small amount of chocolate and even chips are OK for me because I know I'm going to burn it all off. Now I'm not training for a record, I have to be more careful. But counting calories doesn't interest me. I know from experience what to eat and what not to eat. I've always eaten in moderation.

An endurance athlete tends to burn a lot of calories over the miles, running up a mountain or being on a bike or in the ring. You need a great deal of energy. My advice to anyone is not to overeat. A glass of wine now and again is not a bad thing. But it's all about doing these things in moderation. That's worked for me.

I pick up a lot of tips on that from people around me. My sports therapists have advised me over the years and I've got a good basic knowledge now. When I first started training, all those years ago, I'd got it well wrong. I was terrible, eating all the wrong stuff. Cream cakes and fatty foods, fish and chips midday and in the evening too. That was bang out of order.

But, for the first year of going for records, I could get away with a bad diet, I thought. Then, in the second year, 1990, I started to realise that junk food was affecting my performance, both in competition and training. So I had to completely review what I was eating. I've never been a regular drinker. I'll have a shandy or a glass of red wine, which is good for you. And three or four weeks before an event, you stop drinking, except for the odd glass of wine. I don't process alcohol that well anyway: four or five halves of shandy and I'm tipsy. None of my family have been big drinkers.

Yet I move in a circle where there are some heavy drinkers. The sorts of characters my sports disciplines attract are the headbangers and fighters. Ex-boxers and martial artists love the kind of events I did. Working-class guys from rough-and-ready backgrounds. But they're nice, polite, professional people and they're often successful businessmen with their own companies. They're achievers because strength and endurance disciplines and the martial arts are positive sports that attract positive people. And positive people go on to be successful.

Twenty-five years ago an athlete peaked at the age of twenty-eight. Now, it can be thirty-eight. You have athletes making comebacks, coming out of retirement. There are new training programmes which are designed to avoid injury and therapists are available to attend to injuries straight away. Twenty years ago a doctor would say, 'Here's some Paracetamol. Go home and rest.' Now you've got people who specialise in getting you on the road quicker than ever.

I have a lot of faith in my two therapists, Peter Taylor and a Greek guy called Xen Yangou. If I have any back injuries, Xen will massage the problem areas with different herbal oils. I don't delve into the theory of it but, like an aromatherapist, he's able to relax my muscles. He helped me to start training again and produce the goods, and that's all I'm interested in. And Peter also knows all about injury treatments, as well as rehabilitation and remedial and sports massages.

I first shaved my head to help with my training. When you're working hard in the gym and sweating all the time, you're trying to brush perspiration off your head and that gets irritating. You stay a lot cooler if the heat can escape out of the top of your head. Those few degrees make all the difference.

In my record attempts, my job was to perform on the day and the guys around me did their bit. Everyone pooled their resources; it was teamwork. I had to produce the goods, not only for myself but also for the sponsors and the team. Often the team were more nervous than I was. The tension in the changing room just before I attempted a record was almost unimaginable. At that moment I was snappy and aggressive and they were on edge. I was highly charged and the whole team absorbed my mood.

When I did the world-record attempt for press-ups on the backs of the hands for *Record Breakers* in June 2001, I remember there was a lot of tension behind scenes. I'd had to lose a lot of body weight for the event. I was nothing but muscle. It was a speed record and I needed a light body frame plus strength in my arms and wrists. I did seventy press-ups in one minute on the backs of my hands. If I'd been doing normal press-ups, I would have done over a hundred.

The BBC wanted me to get to the venue, at Brindley Square Centre in Birmingham, three hours before the record attempt took place. They had some filming to do for the intro to the event, and the interview for the programme took about an hour and a half to do. It was all done on one very hot day, so I wasted energy hanging around, and I didn't do as many press-ups as I should have.

The interviewer asked me to describe the perfect press-up. I told her that for the backs-of-the-hands press-up, or reverse press-up as they call it now, you place your hands under your chest, just below elbow level, then you come up again with the arms slightly bent. Years ago you used to lock out the arm, but that's now banned because it's bad for the joints. You can get arthritis and tennis elbow from doing that. When you lock out the joint, you think you're resting. It seems easier, but it's not. You're not resting; you're maintaining the position.

I'm able to do press-ups on the backs of my hands because of the flexibility I've gained through the martial arts. I've learnt how to grapple and hold. The first time I heard about reverse press-ups was on the International World Record Holders Association website. These people don't produce books of records; they put all the records on the internet. The Association is based in Leipzig, in Germany, and the website editor is Ralf Laue, who I met when I did my press-ups world record in Flensburg. He's a very clever man. He holds a couple of world memory records. Show him fifty objects and he'll remember them and can repeat them back to you. A real photographic memory.

I did a few world-record runs in a beautiful Irish fishing village called Ballycotton, near Cork. One was the famous Ballycotton ten-mile run in 1993. About three hundred runners entered the race and there was TV coverage of the event. It's a popular international road run, with English and Americans among the competitors. Another time I achieved a speed record: a fifty-mile backpack speed walk round Ballycotton. I also did a sixty-five-mile brick-carrying record there, in September 1994. I could tell you some stories about that one.

For that record I was on my feet for over twenty-four hours. All the locals came out to support me and my Uncle John was there, shouting me on and having a good drink. I was carrying a thirty-pound backpack and a nine-pound weight for a nominated distance. Desi Clifton was at my side, on his bike, and all the Ballycotton officials were lining the route, including the local nurses with their medical back-up. That medical care was very much appreciated because the record attempt was extremely tough and demanding. To be on your feet for over twenty-four hours, non-stop, for sixty-five miles was hard work. The previous record, of sixty-four miles, had been set by my arch rival in endurance record attempts at that time, the American Ashrita Furman.

We followed the Ballycotton ten-mile route the whole time. Over a long period of time like that, you don't get large crowds lining the route, but the locals were great and they came out for me. After about the fiftieth mile I stopped to go to the toilet and collapsed. My heels were covered in blisters and blood. My white socks had changed colour; they were pure red. I was hallucinating and shouting at myself to keep going. But that's part of the mental effort in going for a record.

I was allowed to refresh myself and the local nurses hauled me into the back of a van, changed my boots and socks and powdered my feet. I didn't have the energy to do it myself. But they said to me, 'You've had us on our feet for fifteen bloody hours and if you think we're going back to bed now, you're fucking wrong!' And they threw me out of the van like a bag of spuds. 'Get your arse moving and follow the van!' they shouted.

That spurred me on. I realised the event was more than just about me. Other people were making an effort on my behalf. For a record attempt like that, someone is beside you, monitoring you throughout, but I was out of it by then, following the van on automatic pilot. The lads were shouting at me, winding me up, pushing me on, and I'd give as good as I got, biting back. But I didn't know where I was. It was pitch black and the rain was bucketing down on me. I was drained. I was drinking coffee to keep me awake. I staggered over the finishing line and fell on my knees on the road. Someone picked me up for the photographs, then I was whisked back to where I was staying. After that I was two days in bed. Wrecked.

I said to Desi, 'I'm never going to do this again.' But I was back on another backpack run not long after that. And another time I did a backpack treadmill record live on RTE, the Irish TV channel. Even my Great-Uncle Thomas, aged ninety, turned up at the studio to see that one. Oddly enough, that category of endurance records is the most hotly contested, and it's such a tough event. It needs staying power. Maybe people look at it at first and think it looks easy. It can catch a lot of people out.

The Guinness Brewery Road Race is held in Dublin every year

and I entered it in 1995, carrying a forty-pound backpack. I'd packed this myself, but I thought it might be a bit underweight. The officials of a race always check each backpack carefully on three different sets of scales. My Uncle John was there to support me and I asked him if he had anything in his car that he could shove in the pack to give it weight. He found a lump hammer and reckoned that would do the trick, but, when they came to weigh the backpack, they found I was way over the necessary weight. They took out the lump hammer, and the backpack was underweight. So they put bottles of water in instead, and they got the forty pounds exactly right, to the last ounce.

It was a hard course. There were about two hundred and fifty runners competing from all over Ireland. I thought the course would be flat but it was up and down hill, round the back streets. I thought I was going to lose time, but I made it up. I had cracking support and got coverage on Irish radio. After I'd broken the record, they invited me into the Guinness Brewery bar and presented me with a silver tankard. But that Guinness in Ireland is different from the Guinness we have in the UK. The two halves of Guinness I had were lovely, but they went straight to my head. I definitely felt tipsy.

I recently received the *Strength and Speed Record Book* from the States. As the title implies, the book covers strength and speed records and there's a whole section about me, with photographs of my boxing and martial-arts events. In the 2002 edition of *Guinness World Records* (as *The Guinness Book of World Records* is now called), I've got three record entries. I've been in the book every year since 1990, in different sporting categories.

Press-ups come under the circuit-training category in the record books. Between October 1988 and October 1989 I did 1,500,230 press-ups, but the hardest thing about that world record was having the officials there every day. Without the officials, you can't do the record. The documentation for that event was unbelievable. There must have been about one thousand, two hundred A4 log sheets and witness sheets for that attempt. It made the 1991 edition of *The Guinness Book of World Records*.

The record had been set by a guy in the American forces. I'd seen in it the 1988 edition and thought, Right, I can go for that.' I think he'd done 1,230,000 press-ups in one year, and it was something to go for. But it was twelve months of hard endurance work for about two and a half hours a day, seven days a week. I was travelling around the UK during the attempt, doing the press-ups at different gyms and other venues in various parts of the country. I had one or two days sick during the year, and then I had to make up for the lost press-ups the next day by doing about eight thousand of them.

In September 1991 I went along to Buss-FM Radio in Birmingham to attempt a half-mile backpack treadmill world record. While I was getting changed for the attempt, another guy came along with a backpack to challenge me. He was standing there, probably thinking he was big time, waiting for me to finish. I did the half-mile record with the forty-pound pack on my back and the crowd shouted for the time. Desi yelled back I'd done it in two minutes and fifty-eight seconds. When the guy heard that, he said, 'See ya.' He had his backpack on his bike and he was off. End of challenge.

I've run three full marathons of over twenty-six miles carrying forty-pound backpacks: two in London and one in Wolverhampton. I first decided to do the London Marathon in 1991 for a world-record attempt. Desi was my coach, of course, and two or three other lads from the gym were there to assist me on the day. We mostly used the Clent Hills, a cluster of hills around Birmingham, as a training ground. It's walking country with a lot of steep inclines. I also did a lot of circuit training and martial-arts boxing and pad work for stamina and strength. For any fitness and endurance event you need to work on a variety of disciplines to increase your all-round performance. Every part of you has to co-ordinate at a high level.

You have to train for flexibility as well. This involves stretching techniques to keep calves, back, groin, biceps, triceps and other parts of your body supple. I don't usually get up and start exercising. The gym is a great place for me to 'stretch off' and get flexible. When I was training for a record, I did about two and a half to three hours' training a day.

For about two months before the marathon, I was running around with a seventy-five-pound pack on my back. This meant that on the day, when I put the forty-pound backpack on, it felt a lot lighter, like a feather. And training with a far heavier weight gave me extra strength and power in my back and my legs. I often used this technique of training with an extra load, especially for a backpack endurance event.

There were other people running in the event with backpacks: military teams were running together. But it's much harder to do it as an individual runner. As a team, you can support one another and keep up a certain pace. On your own, you've no one to pace you and no one to support you. Your coach is with you at the start, and then he has to make his way to the finish line. So I didn't see any of my team until the end of the race.

The London Marathon involves thousands of runners and a lot of them are fighting to start off in first place. Because I was running with a backpack on, I barged my way through and marched to the front where the top runners were. I was running against the clock and I had to achieve the fastest time possible with the weight. If I'd stayed at the back, I'd have been delayed. I was about four or five metres back from the main speed runners, ready to go off with them. If anyone had said anything, I'd have said it back. If they'd looked into my eyes, they'd have been looking into a bottomless pit. I was really psyched up. I think my body language said it all.

The psychological preparation for the event was important. Of course, you're nervous the day before and on the day. But in an endurance event like that you're thinking more about the practicalities of the situation: the timing of the event and the backpack. It's important, when you're running marathon distances with a heavy backpack, to make sure your load is comfortable, that it's on straight and not jarring you in any way. You're also checking that the straps of the pack are all right. If they're not, you're finished. If they aren't correctly adjusted, or they're worn and you don't change them, the pack can slip off your back and down your arms. You have to check the laces on your trainers and how they're tied. They mustn't be too tight around the ankles or they restrict the blood supply.

And you have to make sure your feet and thighs are greased with Vaseline, so you don't end up with blisters from friction or grazes. You have to smear Vaseline under your arms as well, because they're going like pistons and the pack is constantly pulling on you. So you're kept busy, kit-checking and looking at technical problems, right up to the last moment.

These are the preoccupations of every experienced marathon runner. They know all about advance preparation. But I've seen people who've never entered a marathon before, running miles and getting sores and not being able to put a T-shirt on afterwards. And they haven't thought about wearing the right socks to reduce friction. Cheap socks can wear through and bring on blisters. Ultra sports socks are pretty good and they absorb the sweat, as all your gear should. Apart from training for an event, your kit list is the most important thing, right down to the size of your shorts. If you've got baggy shorts on, you're going to end up with burns between your legs. And if they're too long, they'll absorb sweat, which not only causes grazing but adds extra weight. You've got to look closely at the material you're wearing. It has to be absorbent without soaking you in sweat.

I preferred shorts to the figure-hugging stretch garments some people wore. It's personal taste, but I liked a bit of airflow to counteract the perspiration. I always wore a running vest. The bergen, which is a specially strengthened army backpack, was full of sand and moulded itself around my back. You had to make sure the sand was dry. The backpack was weighed on an accurate machine before the race and again afterwards. Those are the rules. Anyone can run round a corner and take something out. Often you're carrying an extra pound in weight at the end because the sand has absorbed the sweat on your back. And the water you've been pouring over your head during the race goes straight down to the backpack. I found I lost four or five pounds during an endurance event. It's not just water you lose; your body burns up a lot of fat.

During the run itself, you must drink plenty of liquids along the way. And you have to make sure you don't get caught up in clusters of runners; you could easily trip up or fall and damage your ankle or knee.

I've only ever once checked my pulse during an event: when I was doing a five-hour endurance record. But during another endurance record, at the Royal International Air Tattoo at Fairford, Gloucestershire, a couple of sports therapists did a fitness assessment on me. I already knew John Williams, the former head of the Sports Therapy Department at Solihull College, and he came along with one of my regular therapists, Peter Taylor. I was wired up while I attempted the record, and afterwards they told me my heartbeat hadn't changed throughout the event.

It was a burpees record, which comes under the circuit-training category of fitness and endurance records. I did over three thousand burpees a day for seven days to reach a total of twenty-one thousand, four hundred and nine. This took about three hours every day and my heart rate was checked at the beginning and the end of each session. As I said, it didn't change during the sessions. The heart is a muscle, and mine is well exercised. But I put it down to strength of mind as well as strength of body. It's about focusing as well as maintaining a high level of fitness. I feel strong-hearted. I can feel my energy.

Record breaking wasn't about going for glory. It was about doing the business and having a quiet drink with your team afterwards, then planning for the next record. You'd go home, stretch off, then go down the gym and train hard for the next event. As soon as one record was accomplished, I'd start looking through the record books again.

You don't get out of bed and make records up. You do your research and find out who's done what, and whether it's a breakable record. Then you have to go through a lot of hoops, a lot of admin, to get a record accepted. And you have to find out if the record is of interest to the general public and whether it's going to be accepted within a sporting category. If it isn't, it's looked on as a stunt, a one-off attempt. I'm not really a team player. I've always been more of an individual athlete, like a runner or a boxer. I love the buzz of being one person out there. It's so intense. All the pressure's on me. I've got no one to fall back on or pass the buck to. When I was playing football as a kid and I couldn't get a good kick, it was often someone else's fault. With individual sports, I feel more in control of the event. I can rely on myself and, if something goes wrong, there's no one else to blame. It's all down to me. It's on my shoulders.

When I first got interested in sport, I didn't know where I was going to fit in. I followed mainstream sports until my army days and I'm as fit as I was then. I'm not as fast as I was, but I'm stronger. I'm fitter than any twenty-year-old. I could still beat them on fitness. When I was younger, in the Junior Paras, I could move like a whippet. But not now, I'm too muscular. I weigh about two stone more than I did. As you get older, you put on a pound here and there.

We all did press-ups in PT lessons at primary school but they're considered a minority category in sport. But now, these kinds of disciplines are gaining in popularity, especially at a competitive level. There are keep-fit challenges, there's Britain's Fittest Man, Europe's Fittest Man and other events which are sponsored by sports companies.

I wasn't so interested in fitness competitions; I was more interested in going for world records. If it was a recognised world title in any of my categories and it was in *Strength and Fitness Book* or *The Guinness Book of World Records* or on the International Record Holders Association website, I was interested. This last organisation is just as strict about its paperwork as Guinness is.

Record breaking was no harder for me at the end of my career than it was ten or fifteen years earlier. Being an endurance athlete, you mature. The older you get, the better you get; as I said, it's strength of mind as well as body. You get a lot of endurance athletes in their forties now. I'll continue to train for half marathons and triathlons, but I'm not interested in coming first. I just want to do the competitions to see what they're like. And I won't have to worry about de-training after a career at the top; I'll continue to exercise my heart muscle in competitions.

During my career I wasn't always the one who found records to challenge. Sometimes I was approached by others to try for a record, as I was with the Warlords Kumite World Title. I only had twenty-four hours to get ready for that one, but my mind was already prepared. I only had to slip into a competitive gear, and that was easy because going for a world record always excited me. It was always a challenge; I was always inspired.

CHAPTER 12

STRENGTH AND STAMINA

SOMETIMES I WAS ABLE to go round an endurance course in advance to inspect it, or take a look round a hall and see the equipment in place for a record attempt. But you can't always check a place out, particularly if the event is in another country. When I competed in Germany in July 2000, I had no idea what the venue would be like. I've done half a dozen record attempts outside the UK, and being abroad often gave me an extra buzz. Being in another land, I felt I had to prove myself. People were watching me; I was new and I was something different.

The trip to Flensburg was set up by the German Record Holders Association. To get into that elite group you have to be a Guinness World Record Holder. Then they invite you to their events, which they organise for different types of athletes, such as strong men and endurance athletes.

The venue was packed. It was a brilliant turnout, with a couple of thousand spectators. There were over twenty record holders there, from different Guinness categories. They came from all over the world and I was there, representing Great Britain. Desi Clifton and Anthony McCann, another team assistant, came with me. We had to leave Birmingham at three o'clock in the morning and I drove us down to Stansted Airport for our flight at just after six am. After we arrived in Germany it was another two and a half hours' drive in a minibus. All in all, I'd been up since two in the morning and we didn't get to Flensburg, on the border with Denmark, until nearly midday.

When we contacted the promoter to say we'd arrived, he said, 'You're on at two o'clock.'

I said, 'No I'm not. You've got it wrong. I'm on tomorrow at two o'clock.'

'No, I haven't,' he said. 'It's this afternoon at two o'clock.'

We had one hour to get ready: for me to put on my kit and get down there for the world-record attempt. I was wrecked after all the driving and flying but I had to produce the goods. The stage was massive, right in the middle of the main shopping area. There was a Norwegian strong man on before me. He was a lovely bloke. He broke a world record, pulling a truck and a train. He was really strong. Then I went on and did my record and the crowd was great. I think the organisers were a bit worried because they'd had some trouble with an English athlete who'd behaved arrogantly at a previous event. Apparently the audience had ended up throwing bottles at him.

But the crowd was brilliant, shouting me on and counting me down in German, which I didn't bloody understand. The officials from the German office of *The Guinness Book of World Records* were first-rate and different events took place over the whole weekend. I broke the world record for press-ups on the backs of hands: four hundred and twenty-five press-ups in thirty minutes. I've since beaten that record. I did six hundred and eighty-nine press-ups on the backs of my hands at Digbeth, in Birmingham, in March 2001, but that's now been beaten by a Croatian athlete.

It's easy enough to stay informed about world records. There are various associations which post records on the news sections of their websites. I check in regularly, even now, to update myself on different events.

One of my most memorable record attempts was the twenty-four-hour press-ups record at the Holiday Inn in Birmingham in May 1989. I was pretty scared about that one, keeping going for twenty-four hours. I didn't think I was going to make it. But I had a good team around me. We worked out the average number of press-ups I had to do in an hour, which was around fifteen hundred, and I was allowed to rest for five minutes every hour. In the end I clocked up thirty-seven thousand, three hundred and fifty press-ups. Tired isn't the word, both physically and mentally. I'd trained for four months before the event and the highest number of press-ups I'd managed in training was around ten thousand. It was unbelievably tough. It's the kind of record you only want to do once. But, as long as my name got into *The*

Guinness Book of World Records, I was happy. And it did, in the 1990 edition.

That time Desi Clifton, John McBean and Wayne Bernstein were with me. I've got to admire Desi for his staying power. He's been through a lot of pain with me. I've attempted records where it's been so close that we've thought I wasn't going to make it. Several, in fact. It must have been a relief for him when I did this one.

Desi's very involved with sport; he's a junior football coach. He has a Football Association Club Manager's Diploma and trains a team on the west side of Birmingham. I'm sure he uses the knowledge and experience he's gained working with me to assist with his other coaching.

Right through my thirties, I was still able to break some records by comfortable margins. I put that down to constant training. Even when I had a long break between challenging world records, I kept up my training. To keep yourself at a good level of fitness, you really have to train three or four times a week. This involves a couple of half-hour runs, as well as circuit training.

If you want to go in for world-record attempts in fitness and endurance, you must make sure you're properly prepared. Preparation is the most important thing. You must toughen up your body for an event. You must also have a good training team around you. You have to train hard for a long time before you attempt an ultra world fitness and endurance challenge. But don't kid yourself; don't enter events in which you could injure yourself.

Fitness and endurance training is a lot different from training for a half marathon, which is one sport only. The ultimate fitness athlete must have a strong mind so that he can go any distance, and a high threshold of pain so that he can overcome anything that's hurting. But, at the same time, he has to be able to listen to his body.

I say 'he', but more and more women are becoming record holders in fitness and endurance events now. One girl broke the women's record for press-ups at my gym in 2001. She was a Norwegian who was studying for a degree at Birmingham University. She's definitely up and coming and is recognised by the American Record Book Association. These kind of women's events are starting to become popular in America and Germany. The German Record Holders Association has a lot of women athletes in its organisation who've done press-up events, and it promotes them very well.

People who are over fifty are coming to my gym for training, and that's good to see. It's a gap in the market that should be promoted and expanded. Fitness gyms and health companies should look at the needs of this growing section of the community. There should be reduced rates for pensioners to get them in the door, and also for fifty-somethings because they're the next pensioners. Some of the top gyms are very expensive and not everyone in their fifties is on a managing director's salary. Some people have been made redundant and can't find another job because of their age. But they want, or need, to get fit.

I've been on a few courses for instructors run by the National Coaching Foundation, which cover techniques for winning, such as goal setting. I'm a great believer in accumulating knowledge, so any courses that come up, be it in fitness or the martial arts, I'll go on them. You can always learn something on a course that will make you a better athlete and coach, and you should update yourself regularly in different disciplines. I also read the sports magazines to get different ideas and learn about new training techniques.

One of the most important qualities a coach can have is to be a good listener. In addition you need to have the communication skills to be a good motivator. A good coach should also have a high level of knowledge and experience, though unfortunately that's not always the case. Sometimes sports enthusiasts decide to become instructors, but while they can do the sport themselves, they lack the expertise to pass on that skill. There should be some kind of incentive to encourage a champion athlete into coaching, so he can pass on his unique experience and knowledge effectively.

I've coached one or two people who I've felt had great potential, but I haven't had the time myself to drive them. That would take a lot out of my day. They come to Staminas to improve themselves and then, hopefully, they'll go back to their own gym and take their work further. But there are still not enough sports facilities to go round. National Lottery funding has helped a bit, but more could be done.

Fitness and endurance events can last for anything up to twenty-eight hours. That's how long I was on my feet for a speed walk in 1998, carrying a twenty-pound backpack and a nine-and-a-half-pound weight in a nominated hand. The course followed the

Grand Union Canal. We started in the centre of Birmingham, where the canal begins, and went out to Lower Shuckburgh, about forty miles away, and back.

We started to wonder, 'Had we picked the right route?' We knew the first twenty miles out of Birmingham, along the canal, was flat. But we hadn't looked beyond that. There were inclines and hills, up and down, and the terrain was rough. The footpaths at the side of the canal had small bricks as footholds. When you've been doing miles and miles of these footpaths with a twenty-pound backpack, the impact on the knees and hips is considerable. Twenty-five or thirty miles into the record and I'm thinking, Bloody hell! This is going to be hard. Then it started raining. Late at night, no light. We were trudging through mud, so balance came into it.

The course was exactly seventy-seven miles, three hundred and fifty yards. It was a long and tough one. My mind started playing tricks on me. I was trying to stay awake and I had visions of people coming at me, like shadows out of the mist. I was hallucinating. I imagined people being there, and they weren't. But the team were with me: different pacers at different stages of the course. They were a great team that day. But one of the pacers, a former boxer, a very fit guy, was actually cracking up after about ten hours. It was getting to him. He was shouting and moaning in the rest van, saying he couldn't stand it, it was doing his head in. But I think someone said to him, 'Listen, Paddy's in this for twenty-eight hours and you're moaning after ten.' The guy shut up then.

I was in bits, both mentally and physically, on that course. My body took a real pounding, and the pressure I put on myself to succeed left me psychologically drained. Something like that really knocks you out for a while. No one understands that unless they've actually done it. You can tell someone about it and they can give you sympathy, but they can't imagine it. During some events you're eating and sleeping while you're on your feet. For two or three weeks afterwards you want to be very quiet and repair yourself.

My world record in 1989, for the most press-ups in twenty-four hours, was another tough event. The record had stood at about thirty-five thousand and was held by an athlete from Hong Kong. He only held the record for two weeks. I took it off him with thirty-seven thousand, three hundred and fifty press-ups. I'm sure he was pissed off about that.

That record put me on the road to ultra endurance challenges. I got the taste for putting my head on the block. I'd trained by doing eight to ten thousand press-ups a day. The arms are well pumped up then, and the secret is to have a light body weight. You've got to be compact. I made sure my body weight was down. It wasn't necessary to diet; I burnt off the body fat while I was training. I have a high metabolic rate because I'm always training.

Ultra endurance records are becoming popular throughout the world. But I would say that anyone who wants to go in for these fitness and endurance challenges must be prepared to experience the physical extremes. If you haven't trained long and hard, it's a shock to the body. From what I can see of the background of endurance athletes, they've been involved in sport from an early age, so their stamina has developed over the years. A lot of these athletes, but not all, also have a military background, which has given them self-discipline. One or two have also come from deprived backgrounds. Maybe hunger for success is a motivation. These people want to make something of their lives.

I didn't come from a deprived background, but I certainly didn't come from a privileged one. I had a turbulent childhood and a tough time at the schools I went to because I was always involved in fights. I won a lot and I lost a lot, and that toughened me up. From an early age kids wouldn't fight me one to one: I was always having to take on two or three at a time. They must have seen me as a threat. It made me hungry to prove myself, but also very wild. I could be nasty to those who crossed me. I never took prisoners.

And I dabbled in alcohol when I shouldn't have. Alcohol was bad news for me. I was never an alcoholic, but drink fired me up. A couple of beers and bang! It blew my sockets. Dangerous stuff. It turned me from Jekyll into Hyde. It turned the skills I had on the judo or martial-arts mat, or in a boxing ring, into the weapons of a nut case. I'd hit anyone: bouncers, doormen, and I'd knock them out. If a gang was having a fight, I'd jump in the middle of it. I was the ringleader. I was a headbanger. Absolutely crazy, when I look back. Maybe the booze simply enhanced my general mood at that time.

Would I behave like that now? I would, if anyone crossed me. I've still got that basic reaction. It's part of my personality; it's in my make-up. It's in my bones and in my brain. I'll give you an example: last night I went down to a gym in Birmingham. Some bloke kept nudging my leg in the jacuzzi. He did it four or five times. I didn't know what his game was. He was with another guy and I think he was doing it on purpose. You nudge someone once, but you don't keep doing it. When I got out of the jacuzzi, I kicked him in the leg. 'I'm sorry,' I said. 'You all right, are you?' I smiled at him, and walked away with a glance over my shoulder. He knew.

It's a reflex. Touch me and I'll touch you – bang! I've always reacted; it's inbuilt. It's survival of the fittest. It's dog eat dog out there. If you want to survive, you've got to be the toughest on the block. You've got to be a Rottweiler, not a poodle. If people make it awkward for you, you make it awkward for them, physically or mentally. If they're playing mental games, don't get mad, get even.

Even today, if I go out for a drink with the lads and there's a problem, I'll have a go. The time I was in Ireland is a typical example of this. A couple of Guinnesses and I was ready to sort out the situation. It was the other guy who didn't turn up. I was ready and raring to go at five o'clock in the morning, with a balaclava and a big stick, to sort out somebody I didn't know who was beating up a woman I'd never met.

And I'd do that today. If someone needed help, I'd give them support. If not physically, I'd do it verbally. I'd tell them how to approach the problem and solve it. And if they couldn't do that, if they couldn't defend themselves or their premises, I'd tell them how to sort it out physically.

This attitude comes from my childhood. It's how I grew up. A lot of your attitude will depend on how hard you had it as a child. You've got to fight your way out of the ghetto. I always come back to that moment when I was about four or five, when I looked up and said I wanted to do something with my life. I wanted to be something, although at that age I had no clear image of what that would be. Whatever I do, I make a success of it.

Fitness is the fastest-growing activity for all age groups. It has a social side to it too. People make new friends. I've made a lot of my friends that way. A high percentage of my friends are involved in sport, whether it's weightlifting or running, boxing or the martial arts. If you're committed to a sports career, your social life is going to stem from that.

I called my gym Staminas Boxing Self-Defence Centre because it seemed appropriate to the level of training I give my students, how far I push them. And it connects with the title of my website: www.stamina4life.co.uk. Although Holly Lane is in a nice area, the groundsman and steward keep a constant eye on the Sports and Social Centre and its playing fields. You get a lot of youths wandering about. I tend to have a chat with them, so they stay away from the Centre. Sometimes it's been more than a chat.

I've had to stop gangs vandalising my gym in the past. I've caught them trying to break windows. The Sports and Social Centre is a family club and I'm part of that club. One time I picked some of them up by the scruff of the neck and escorted them out. I said to them, 'I know where you live. If you do that, I'll come round and pour petrol on your cars.' That tends to put the wind up them. They're on drugs and you've got to respond to the situation in a strong way. And it's effective. If you say you're going to go round to their houses and damage their property, they'll think twice. I can always find out where someone lives. It's a case of communication, talking to people. I've lived in Birmingham all my life. I've got contacts underground and overground.

I prefer to rent my gym because I'm never sure if I want to continue in that field. There are other things I want to do. I want to give more courses in other places; I want to travel and meet new people. I don't want to stay still. I want to visit clubs elsewhere. If I had to run a string of gyms, I'd end up pushing paper round a desk all day. I want to spend my time passing on my skills.

But my gym has its social side: it's a good meeting point for all my sports contacts. And it's always been useful for training for record challenges and dan grades in the martial arts. A lot of my friends come from that world. It's become part of my social life, as well as my career. I run a small club with a low membership and I prefer it that way. I only allow a few people to use the place at any one time. I don't have any interest in running a large establishment: I'm involved in too many other things.

I coach members myself, so I see everyone who comes into my gym. We call it squad training. Sometimes I train with the group; sometimes I just stand up front and teach. Training with a group; helps me to stretch myself in fitness and endurance. The squad are chosen because they're all at a certain level and can push one another to new limits. In a mixed-ability group, the best athletes don't get the chance to take their fitness further. The squad are the cream of the athletes, the elite. They helped me and pushed me when I was training for world-record attempts. It was one of the factors that made my record challenges a team event.

These people not only helped me to train but they represented the gym when we turned out for an event. We also have our own sports club awards each year, which helps to motivate people. We lay on a buffet and a disco and we have a trophy for the most improved athlete, and also for skills in the martial arts, boxing and fitness.

My gym is known more for these than for weights or any other kind of training. It's a very basic place, and as soon as you get there, you know you've got to work. No messing about. And I believe very strongly that's where champions are made. It doesn't happen in the glitzy gyms where people read the morning papers while they're sitting on a bike.

At the gym, we're not into detailed conversations about what everyone did at the weekend. We're more likely to get stuck in and bust a gut. That's the kind of training I promote and that's the hard-working atmosphere I've created. There's a yearly fee to cover accident insurance and a session fee which goes towards the equipment. A session lasts for a couple of hours and we train a couple of times a week. Other evenings, I'm involved with other types of coaching. The reason there isn't a large membership at the gym is that I really push people to get the best out of them. The training is tough and only a few people are able to stick at it.

I've had a lot of guys come down who fancy themselves in the gym. They think they're big shots, but they fail to make the grade. They've come from other clubs where they've done boxing and the martial arts, but my club has turned out to be too tough for them. I have a high drop-out rate. It's our workouts: the way we train, the way we operate. Newcomers find it difficult to adapt to our highly disciplined regime. We're very focused. It takes a lot of time and effort to build up a reputation like that. And it's a genuine one.

Because the gym was originally a squash court, you can still see the faded lines on the floor and the ball marks around the walls. Some friends in the building trade helped me put in a boxing ring and rig up the punchbags. We have showers there and basic central heating. Some people followed me to Holly Lane from my old club at the Magnet Centre; the rest have come along just through hearing about the place. Some people, outside the club, have asked to use the place to train. That's basic manners in the sports world: asking the instructor first puts you in his good books. But some have come along and they've been a bit arrogant in their approach, and that doesn't do them any favours.

I can usually spot the athletes who are going to amount to something. Those who have an open mind and take in what they're told. Those who come regularly have the right amount of commitment. I'm not looking for the ones who are best all the time. I'm looking for the ones who try, who put in the effort. They might come last in the physical fitness tests or a sparring session but it's the long haul that counts.

The gym itself could be part of a James Cagney film set: shafts of dusty light picking out the boxing ring and the punchbags. I've put up some pictures of my record challenges, some of my certificates and interviews with magazines as an incentive to new members. Each poster and picture has a story behind it.

Only two of the three punchbags are in use. One has collapsed from constant pounding and needs repairing. The bags are different weights for trying out different punching skills. There's a long one of eighty pounds that we use for power punching. The other is about thirty pounds and thin at the bottom. That's used for upper cuts and kicking and is covered in footmarks. There are two full-length mirrors for shadow boxing and there's a rowing machine. Nothing high-tech.

The beginners' training programme is posted on the wall and includes ground/floor impact blows, explosive power punches, bone-to-bone impact and take downs. The ground/floor impact blows are designed to injure the opponent as much as possible at ground level. Explosive power punches involve bag work and using pads, putting your bodyweight behind your punch, while instruction in bone-to-bone impact shows the student how to smash their bone against someone else's to break it. Take downs are about learning to throw someone on to the floor. For safety, everything is practised in the ring on the mats.

I have my own special combination of boxing and martial-arts techniques; strike skills I've adapted from different disciplines. Close-quarter impact reality strikes involve getting close to someone, violating their air space to defend yourself as much as possible when you're being threatened. A new member might learn all of these moves in the first session, if I think they're learning fast. There are photos on the walls of my students demonstrating how to punch and kick and use elbow, so that others can follow their example.

I grade people for their martial-arts yellow belt at the club. Kumite martial arts includes continuous fighting. Each student is assessed on teamwork, skill, fitness, boxing and basic martial arts. Everyone wears head guards and gum shields, gloves and bandages for their hands and wrists. The grading involves fifteen-minute runs, one hundred burpees, one hundred press-ups, five three-minute rounds of light boxing sparring, ten minutes of non-stop break falls, ten minutes of skilled shadow boxing and five minutes of punch and kick-pad skills.

In addition people get in the ring as many times as they can every week, and the rounds are added up at the end of six months. The three people who've accumulated the highest number of rounds are given a trophy at our sports awards evening. It means that my students have always got challenges when they come to the gym. It helps them improve themselves. And I get into the ring with them and fight them every time. I'm always sparring. I love it.

Regular sparring keeps me fit and I enjoy passing on my skills. It keeps me alert; I'm fighting a variety of people all the time. Paul Jones, my assistant coach, still gets in the ring and he's forty-nine. But when I got write-ups in the local press for record challenges, it tended to put people off coming to the club rather than encourage them. Maybe they felt the standards would be too high for them.

When we do martial-arts sparring, we move the mats to the larger hall in the Sports Centre because the discipline needs more floor space. You have to move around, kicking and punching, using a lot of karate skills, freestyle and judo throwing techniques.

There's a training chart on the wall, showing ways in which you can develop your body – for example, to improve the muscles on your shoulders and behind your neck. We often stand and do exercises on the spot. Before we got the grading system up and running, we held challenges that were similar to the belt gradings. Members had to complete as many press-ups as possible in five minutes, as many burpees as possible in five minutes, as many squat thrusts as they could in that time and as many squats as possible. We included a weight-carrying challenge where people had to run, carrying two heavy bags, forty times, between the two outer lines of the gym hall; two minutes of non-stop bench press-ups; ten two-minute rounds of boxing sparring; twenty minutes of non-stop ground/floor grappling; five minutes using only a straight left punch as many times as possible; and finally five minutes using a straight right punch. All of the exercises were counted and timed.

I've hung thick cardboard on the walls to prevent people banging their heads and injuring themselves. The ring has ten mats of double thickness and the corner posts are wrapped in sponge rubber and tape. In the corner are a pile of kick pads for feet and hands, elbows and knee strikes, and there's a large cupboard of gloves of different sizes. There are skipping ropes, a rack of dumb-bells of different weights, medicine balls, bricks for working out to improve body strength and weightlifting belts. The belts are padded to support the lower back.

A large poster on the wall shows the pressure points on the body. If you struck someone on one of those points, you'd stop them coming at you. The skull, the temple, the bridge of the nose, jaw, collar-bone, the solar plexus, groin, shin and instep, plus the elbow, the base of the cerebellum, the upper back and the small of the back are all pressure points, as are the tops of the thighs and calves and Achilles tendon. You can attack someone using the fore fist, the back fist or bottom fist, one-knuckle fist, middle finger, fore-knuckle fist and the ridge of the hand.

There's one other press cutting on the wall. It's an article about a lad who used to come down to the gym, and trained a lot with me. Nice lad. We used to call him 'Fuzzy'. One night, a few years back, he was in a West Indian nightclub in Birmingham. Whatever he was involved in, that was down to him. The way I heard it, two Yardies, Jamaican gangsters from London, tried to take some jewellery off his friend. Fuzzy jumped in the middle of them and got shot in the head. He died instantly.

My gym holds a lot of memories. I've had European and British champions there, and many established martial-arts fighters have come down and got in the ring. Some of them have pretended they don't know how to box and they've come at me like a bull at a gate and ended up on their arse. Admittedly, I've had a few black eyes out of it; I haven't walked away unscathed. They've come at me to hurt me and I've made sure I've put some manners on them. I've gone for three rounds, then caught them out in the fourth. Bomp! And next minute they're on the ropes. Experience and stamina show through at the end of the day.

Stamina is where I really score. As a fighter, I'm small in stature. I used to get hit a lot on the way in, but I'd wear down my opponent with the body shots and upper cuts. I'd tire them out with my fitness and strength.

Every week I do four or five rounds of kumite sparring, which is martial-arts skills and boxing combined. It's fairly competitive. All students try it on with me. I'm the ultimate challenge for them. They want to come up to that standard. They want to push themselves and they know I train hard. That's why the gym isn't packed with members; my courses are very demanding. Besides, eight or ten people training on a squash court, plus equipment, is enough.

My gym is just a small martial-arts, boxing and fitness club, and I'd like to keep it that way. The courses I run just about cover the rent, so it pays for itself. I used to come to the gym on Sunday mornings for squad training when I was working for my record attempts. Our sparring sessions and physical fitness sessions were at a very high level. The squad are the select few who can keep up with me, who can push me as well as pushing themselves.

My fiancée, Samantha, also comes to the gym. She gets in the ring and spars. It's light-contact stuff, but she's growing in confidence. She's on the punchbags and she's on the kick pads and she's going for her yellow belt. When she met me, she'd done a small amount of basic martial-arts training, but nothing to the standard we have at my gym. It's changed her attitude and her approach to business. Not that she's ever been soft in business, but

CHAPTER 13

BRAINS AS WELL AS BRAWN

IF YOU'RE AN AMATEUR athlete going for world records, you need a lot of time and commitment. Record breaking is a short-term career and, to get where I did, I had to be selfish with my time. I didn't feel my social life was suffering because I was doing what I was interested in, but I think I broke the world record for girlfriends.

Until I met Samantha, I hadn't met a woman who understood the discipline and commitment that was needed for what I was doing. But Samantha did understand. The lady had had her own careers. She'd been a successful pop singer in her twenties and then, once again, a winner with her telecommunications business. She has my outlook, my focus. To achieve what she has, she's had to have her own sense of commitment and staying power. She also comes from a similar background to mine: she's had it hard. She comes from a different part of Birmingham but her family life was just as tough as mine. But that's another story.

During my lean years I had to sort out some troublesome people for others. When business acquaintances weren't paid the money they were owed, I had to go round and see the other party and get them to pay up. I usually said something like, 'You've got to pay, or your car's gone.' But that was a long time ago, before I had a full-time job. It took me a while to realise that if I didn't keep myself occupied, I'd get involved in something I might regret. And it was getting that way.

I could see I was getting temperamental and unnecessarily violent. One night I came out of a side road near my gym as another driver was coming down the road. He must have been in a bad mood. I was doing everything right: signalling before I turned right, plenty of distance between us. But he must have taken a dislike to the car I was driving. He kept flashing his lights and sticking his fingers up at me. I thought, What's he doing that for? and carried on. The guy pulled into the side of the road, so I turned back to see if I knew him. I parked and got out and the guy reversed in his car to cut me up. He was a big guy. And I thought, What the bloody hell is going on here?

The guy got out and said, 'Do you know who I am?'

'No, I don't,' I said. It was a David and Goliath situation all over again.

'You cut me up,' he said.

'No, I didn't,' I told him. 'I was in the right. There was plenty of space.' Which there was. But he came at me and I thought he was going to strike me. So I hit him with an upper cut and he landed on the bonnet of the car and slid down it.

I remember thinking, I'm on a main road here. People are driving past. I'm round the corner from my gym and people know me in this area. Jesus Christ, I've got to get out of here.

Meanwhile the bloke had picked himself up off the floor. He said to me, 'Do you realise I'm a police officer?'

I looked at him. 'You wouldn't come at me with a punch if you were a police officer,' I said. 'You're lying to me. I'm not stupid. If you're a police officer, I'll follow you to the police station.' So I followed him for about ten minutes and I must have scared him. He ended up driving into a council estate, and parked on a driveway. Whether it was his or not, I don't know.

That evening I did think, This has got to stop. But sometimes you've got to react in life. If I hadn't hit him, he would have hit me. And that's how it's been in ninety-nine per cent of the confrontations I've been in. I've been right to defend myself. I've never purposely provoked people.

Another serious moment for me was 14 November 1998, a couple of weeks after I got the European record for the thirteen-mile half marathon in Wimbledon, London. I was in a city-centre pub in Birmingham, drinking with an acquaintance. We finished our drinks and decided to get a taxi home. We walked up to Small Heath, near Birmingham City football ground, to find a taxi. On the other side of the road, an Asian youth was standing there. He crossed the road and came towards us. He demanded a cigarette. I don't smoke and I told him to get on his bike. I said, 'We're waiting for a taxi,' and I thought that was it.

But he went to get something out of the lapel of his coat. I thought it was a knife. I hit the guy and he ended up in the middle of the road. He got up and I could see his eye was cut. I still thought he was going to stab me because, at that time, there were a lot of white youths being attacked by Asian gangs in that part of Birmingham. But, as I'd struck him, suddenly a number of Asian blokes had appeared from the shadows. About fifteen or sixteen of them. I was surrounded.

I remember one of them: he had a bald head and he carried an extendable metal baton, just like the ones the police use. The guy who'd been drinking with me was about six foot one, but he melted into a shop doorway. If he'd been with me and been verbally strong, I reckon we could have swung it. I wasn't looking for trouble, I wanted to go home. One of the Asians said to me, 'What have you done to my friend's eye?'

I said, 'Well, he came over to me looking for trouble.' By this time one or two of the gang had got behind me and were lobbing bricks at me. Then I got hit by a bottle. I've still got a scar about four inches long from that. Someone picked up a large plastic delivery basket and threw it at me. I said, 'Well, you're throwing stuff at me, but I'm not going on the floor for you.' By now my eye was cut and I was bleeding at the back of my head. 'If you all put your weapons down,' I told them, 'I'll fight you one by one.'

But they wouldn't have it. So I thought I'd better get out of there. I called to the guy I'd been with, who was still in the shop doorway, 'You'd better go,' and I got ready to do a runner. I knew I had to get out fast. I was surrounded by grown men and there were bricks and bottles coming at me. I couldn't have taken much more of it; the blood was going into my eye. As I went to exit, the bald guy with the truncheon got behind me and hit me with it. Down I went on the floor, holding my head in pain. That was the signal. The lot of them closed in and jumped up and down on my body.

After they'd trampolined on me, I came out of it with a dislocated hip. My leg was hanging off. When the police arrived, they took one look at me and thought I was drunk and disorderly. They thought I'd crossed the road and fallen over.

I needed a major operation on my hip. The surgeon put it right, thank God. The operation was a success. But I woke up the next morning with tubes coming out of my nose and mouth and nurses all around me. My face was a real mess. My head was shaved at the back and I had stitches down to the eyebrow. I was hospitalised for two weeks and that gave me time to think about the cowards who could only hunt in packs with weapons and jump on people. I came out of that place with a lot of anger and bitterness inside me.

After the operation, I needed physiotherapy. A dislocated hip is worse than a broken leg. The specialist said to me, 'Paddy, we know what you do. We know about your world records. Forget about your career now. It's not going to happen. You're retired now.'

I said, 'OK then.' But something in my head said, 'No, that's not right.' I'm a fighter.

The two weeks in hospital were up, and they were going to keep me in for another week if I failed a simple assessment test. Could I get up on my crutches? Could I go down the corridor? Could I come back? The problem is, after two weeks on your back, your balance goes. But I'm not a quitter. I got up, went up and down the corridor on my crutches – bump, bump, bump. I got myself released and was out of the door with a friend by two in the afternoon. But I had to stay home for about a week. Every time I tried to get up, it took me about five minutes to get off my backside. I was still in a lot of pain.

I saw a couple of osteopaths, Ray Norwood and John Williams, who are good friends of mine. The specialist at the hospital had told me to rest but these two guys said, 'No. Swim. The water will take your weight.' And I had hot baths every day to get the circulation going, and oils massaged into my hip and Raljex sprayed on the afflicted area. The osteopaths gave me laser treatment on my leg for about three months and I sat in the jacuzzi at the Living Well Centre in the National Exhibition Centre, basking in the bubbles. I was determined to come out of this as strong as I'd been before. I biked and swam and got treatment from Ray and John three or four times a week. But it was costing me money and I had no money coming in.

I went back to see the specialist a few times and he was amazed. He gave me a strength test for my legs and wanted to know how come I was healing so quickly. I could raise my leg and push out; I could have pushed through walls. I didn't tell him I was seeing osteopaths because the specialist wanted my body to heal itself in its own time. But this other treatment worked for me and I rate it highly. Osteopaths have helped me in the past with vertebrae injuries and, to me, they're the specialists for problems like that.

Seven months after I was attacked, in May the following year, I did another world-record attempt. I was back on course again, training and running five miles in the Royal British Legion Runathon with a fifty-six-pound pack on my back. The record is going in the 2002 edition of *Guinness World Records*.

There was a police sergeant who was involved in the investigation of the attack who occasionally came to my martial-arts classes at the Fox Hollies Leisure Centre. 'I heard you'd been attacked,' he said. 'We thought you'd had a skinful.' They'd had to send the police round to see me at the hospital and amend all their paperwork. I think someone got carpeted for assessing the situation wrongly. But the coppers were supportive in the end. One of them said to me, 'If you want to go back and sort it out, we'll make sure we're not on shift at the time.' That cheered me up. That attack was supposed to signal the end of my sports career, but I broke many records after that.

I came into record busting with a tough event, and I went out with one of the hardest challenges of my career. Not that records I've gone for have ever been easy. I've always set out to test and prove myself. Any challenge that was thrown at me in the past, I've risen to it. I trained for the moment and achieved the record. That's the type of athlete I was. I didn't confine myself to one category of sport. I could adapt to different types of training for different sporting events. And I was able to adjust mentally. A lot of it is about mindset. It's about self-belief. You think about achieving the record while you're training. You're rehearsing the moment, adapting your body and your mind.

The 'will to win' kicks in the first time you look at a record some other athlete has just achieved or broken, either in a record book or in the press. The first thing I always thought when I learnt about a record, even before I left the gym or newspaper shop, was: Can I beat that? I was already turning the possibility over in my mind. Other people read record books out of interest. When I looked at a record book, I was thinking, I can do that. I can beat that one. Some people look at a record, and think. When I looked at a record, I knew. And that's a different level of self-belief.

I'd always read record books in this way. I was looking to beat numbers not just in one discipline, but in about seven different categories. There was circuit training, which is a combination of one-arm press-ups and squat thrusts; there was the martial arts and kumite fighting. Boxing was another category; brick-carrying records were another and distance walking another. There were also multi-terrain challenge events, taking on hills and mountains, and coal-bag and log-carrying events which were more about strength. The speed and stamina records, where I did one event after another, such as in the World Speed Versatility Record I broke in 1991, involved challenges such as weightlifting, squat thrusts, backpack running and coal-bag carrying.

Achieving these world records took a lot out of me: the planning and the paperwork, organising tickets, meeting people and the press, and training at the same time. And I needed one or two days where I could just rest my body, especially after the injuries I got while training.

It was hard work and I had to manage most of it myself. I never had a proper manager. I had to deal with people, meetings and organising events, but I learnt how to negotiate and delegate. And there was a sports club in Birmingham that let me use their equipment for training, as well as giving me therapist treatment. They were very supportive during the last three years of my career.

And I was lucky with my team. When I got to an event, they'd run around sorting things out and leave me to concentrate on the record. They were very loyal, and I couldn't have had a better bunch of blokes. One record attempt that was badly organised, and it wasn't down to us, was at RAF Cottesmore, where they were holding the Royal International Air Tattoo. We arrived the day before. I was due to attempt a world record of five hours of alternate squat thrusts the next day. But they didn't have any beds for us, so my team and I had to sleep in a tent, which was a bit rough.

If you're going for a world record and you're put in a damn tent, it's frustrating. The organisers knew we were coming, and they could have arranged some accommodation. The next day I achieved the national record with six thousand, six hundred and ninety-six squat thrusts in five hours, but I could have done a lot better if the whole thing had been better planned.

I never earned a lot of money with my sport but I'm about to develop the business side of that now. I want people to respect me as they did when I was breaking records, and I'll be as tough in business as I was in sport. I'm not saying I know something other people don't know, but I'm not about to be trampled on. In my line of sport I was a one-off. No one can match my experiences in so many different disciplines. And it's all noted in the record books. It's not just talk, it's action.

I've been in *The Guinness Book of World Records* every year, for different records, since 1990. The records I broke in the late eighties took some time to be authenticated and processed. Guinness get sent thousands of records a year and the new records don't always make the publication date for the book. Sometimes I've had more than one entry in the same year. Nineteen ninety-one was probably my best year: I had six entries in the book, plus a photograph of one of my record challenges.

This is probably a good moment for me to change direction in life but, at the same time, keep the basics in place. My knowledge and experience and the contacts I've made in the sports world are going to bring other challenges, without me punishing myself physically. I've had the pain many times. Now it's time to enjoy keeping fit and pass on my know-how to others.

To help fund myself during the lean days of my career, I applied for a job with the Prince's Trust. I became a team leader for them, working with young offenders. I spent the first twelve months at Solihull College, then moved around other colleges as a team leader. I was working with people who'd just come out of prison or been expelled from school. My job was to put them on various training programmes to help them develop basic skills, or on residential courses to give them another chance in life. But there was a high burnout rate among staff, partly because of the kind of client we were dealing with. Being with fifteen people from a disadvantaged background from nine to five every day can take a lot out of you. Team leaders tended to last from six to twelve months. I lasted two and a half years. But I didn't enjoy the last six months at all.

I had a lot of disagreements with people towards the end of my time with the Prince's Trust. I felt burnt out and I didn't think I was getting support from a particular manager. I went off sick with a bad back for a couple of months, but I still managed to keep up my training. I went in for the Warlords Kumite World Title, and won it. The tournament was covered in the press and, of course, this got back to my bosses. I was told to report back to work and explain myself.

I went in, put my hand up and said, 'Well, it's one of those things, isn't it?' But they were annoyed because they'd been concerned about me. They didn't want to lose me because they were short of team leaders, but they put me on a final warning. I started back at work but I had the feeling that some of the management wanted to get rid of me, there and then, so I began to lose interest in the job. I'd been promised some promotion but it never came. Suddenly I'd had enough.

One day I had a heated discussion with the management. I thought they were weak and I told them so. We had a major disagreement about funding and I made my feelings known pretty aggressively. I remember telling one manager I thought he was a sneak and that I didn't trust him. Next thing, I was up before a disciplinary committee, and not long after that I was asked to leave. But there'd been an upside to the job. For the Trust's twenty-fifth anniversary, the top team leaders were invited to Buckingham Palace to see the Queen, the Duke of Edinburgh and Prince Charles. The historical setting was magnificent and we watched the presentations for the awards. The Queen looked very small, surrounded by security men. Tony Blair was there; the buffet was superb and we had a cracking time. I stood next to the refreshments table and drank every drink that was offered. And left Buckingham Palace pissed.

I first met Samantha in a pub disco called Hemingway's. She was with her previous boyfriend at the time. I think I said to her something like, 'What are you doing with him?' and got him to leave. It's dog eat dog in this world.

But she was thinking of leaving the guy anyway. And, a couple of months later, she did. During that period, between my first meeting her and starting to go out with her, I sometimes met up with her brother, Billy, and occasionally Samantha was with him. One evening when we were all together, the conversation got around to the fact that Samantha was trying to lose some weight. I bet her brother £500 that she'd lose weight if I was training her. And she lost the weight, no problem.

To be honest, the bet was more in the nature of a joke. I didn't think she'd take the offer seriously, but she phoned and came down to my gym for one-to-one training. Pretty soon I was teaching her boxing and the martial arts, partly to get her fit and partly to build up her confidence to defend herself if she was ever under threat. Samantha has verbal confidence anyway, because she's a successful businesswoman. I admire and respect her for that. She's a fighter by nature. She's had a few turbulent experiences in the business world and she's come out of those as a winner.

You could say we've got a similar outlook on life. We've had comparable experiences, in a way. Samantha was an entertainer before she was a businesswoman and my line of sport was a form of entertainment too. I wasn't a personality standing on a stage, singing or telling jokes; Samantha had to talk to people and look good. But I was an athlete and I still had to perform in public, even if I'd got bruises all over my face.

When we first met I was working as a coordinator for the Millennium Volunteers, which is a government initiative unit of the Department of Education. This scheme was set up for youngsters aged between sixteen and twenty-four who were out of work. They were sent on courses to help motivate them and they were found jobs in the community, and that looked good on their CVs. I was something of a mentor for these young people, who'd been sent to us by sixth forms and colleges or employment services. Some of them were teenagers who'd been expelled from school or college, sometimes they were young people who were unable to get a job for some reason – for example, because they were on drugs.

My job with the Millennium Volunteers was based in

Stratford-upon-Avon, where we had an office on a barge. This barge had been donated to a youth club by various charities. During the day, pensioners used to come and sit and have a cup of tea there while I sat in my office and interviewed prospective Millennium Volunteers. Obviously a high percentage of candidates had police records and I would put them through a selection process that included form-filling and an interview. You had to be careful where you sent drug dealers and arsonists; I had to make sure I didn't send any arsonists to work in a paper mill. I'd put someone like that on a farm in the middle of nowhere and let him clean up horse shit and cow shit. It'd still look good on his CV.

South Warwickshire was my patch. I was driving around Alcester and Kenilworth and over to Stratford-upon-Avon, nice parts of the world. I could handle the responsibility but I wasn't happy with all the driving. Samantha reckoned I should leave and start using my knowledge and experience to do coaching again. It was she who encouraged me to make my first video. She tends to underline ideas that are brewing in my head. We think in the same way. We're supportive of each other. We're a good team.

When she was in her early twenties, Samantha was a singer in a pop group called Volcano. I didn't follow the charts but her brother, Billy, always spoke highly of his sister's singing. The group was a trio: two of the members came from Norway, and they recorded on the D Construction record label. In July 1994, one of Samantha's songs got to number thirty-two in the English charts and was number four in Japan. She did a lot of public appearances with different celebrities and stars and toured in other countries, so she understood the world of PR and promotion, even before she started her own business.

Samantha began singing when she was sixteen. At twenty-eight she decided her pop career wasn't progressing and she called it a day. But it was a hard choice for her to make. Her career had been like mine: working hard to achieve a polished performance, getting people to look at what you're doing, plus enjoying the successes. It upset her, for a while, to let go of all that investment in time and effort and she began to let herself go a bit, physically. She'd always been a fit person, but once she stopped singing, she had a down period. After we'd trained for a while, she got that ambition back and the drive to go forward. Now she trains at a gym in Solihull and comes once a week to the boxing and martial-arts sessions at my gym, where she's punching and kicking for her grading.

When she first started martial-arts training with me, she says she felt like a clumsy lump. After two weeks I showed her a break fall and got annoyed because all she could do was stand and laugh. You need to be able to fall properly when you're attacked so that you don't break any arms or legs. I set her a target to get her yellow belt and I saw her focus on that immediately. Now she's into the boxing and her skills have greatly improved.

When I'm in the gym I'm an instructor, an athlete. When I'm at home I'm completely different. I keep my life in separate compartments. I enjoy teaching, particularly at advanced levels such as the bodyguard courses I run. I couldn't do gym instruction on a regular basis. I'd find it too boring now. I've cranked up a level and I enjoy teaching other instructors. That's the top of the ladder for me, and I've had to work for that. Some of the lads I teach are ex-forces: ex-Royal Marine Commandos and ex-Paras with a similar background to mine. They're high-level instructors themselves and it's great to know they're learning from me. They've become instructors but I've taken those skills to a competitive level. You learn a lot more when you do something as a fighter, rather than just getting your gradings.

Gradings are hard enough, but doing competitions as well gives you hands-on experience. You pick up techniques when you're actually in a competition. When you've been penalised by a referee or told you can't do that again, you have to get it right. I've had my fingers and nose broken in competitions, as well as in pub brawls. But for me, to be a real fighter is to get in the ring. At that moment you're sober: no drugs or alcohol, and you're there to inflict as much pain on someone as possible. When you're drunk, you can't get that right. You're dehydrated; you lose your power and your skills and your focus. But for two men to get into a ring, who've trained for that moment and who are prepared for punishment, that's a different level.

I take my coaching seriously. I feel proud when Samantha tells me she wouldn't have got as far as she has in the martial arts with any other instructor. She's learnt punching techniques and now has strength in her arms. She'll push someone when she's having a laugh, and they'll go flying. Most of all, the training has been good for her confidence. She feels a lot safer. She knows the moves, the kicks and the punches, and she walks down the street using the right body language. And we know body language can put people off thinking about mugging you. Even so, if you don't like a situation, get out of it as quickly as possible. Don't hang around to be a hero, or heroine.

Samantha trains at boxing and freestyle martial arts, which is a combination of karate and unarmed combat. Unarmed combat is about palm strikes and elbow strikes. Nowadays the martial arts don't always focus on one way of fighting. In the last ten years the sport has completely changed. A lot of martial-arts organisations are starting to realise their particular method isn't right for everyone. Many are bringing in various techniques from other styles of fighting, and they call this new approach freestyle.

My fiancée understood the pressures that were on me when I was challenging a record, and she'd step back and let others take over. She knew about the build-up of adrenalin for a record attempt. It looked easy on the day, but she saw how the pressures beforehand could affect me. She was watching me when I got sick or low. She knew from her own stage performances that I was as worried about letting myself down as I was about letting down other people. She knew there was more than training to achieving a record; she saw how the build-up affected every part of my life.

To be number one, you don't just get out of bed in the morning and become number one. It takes more than natural ability; you have to push that ability to the max to get one hundred and fourteen world records. Samantha saw me in my low periods, after an event. I could get a bit snappy and she'd keep out of the way for a day or two. You get so high after challenging and achieving a record that there's only one way to go while your body's repairing itself. But you don't realise you're being short with people.

We've both been role models, in different branches of entertainment. We've both had young people look up to us. We've both been under the microscope in that respect. Samantha's a role model for her family as well. Her nephews and nieces go around proud as Punch, talking about what she's done. And I get on really well with her family. Sadly, her mother died just before we got together, but I get on like a house on fire with her father and her two brothers. I think this is because we've had similar childhoods: working class and down to earth. We mickey-take a lot too. Often I'll give Samantha some stick and she gives as good as she gets. It can be frightening! But I love her for it. She's a good woman and I'm sure we'll go on, from strength to strength.

What was different in my life towards the end of my record-breaking career was that I had a partner. I hadn't had that domestic commitment before. I began to realise I was ready to settle down and start a family with someone who understood the pressures I had in my career. But Samantha got upset when she saw what I went through each time. She told me to lift the pressure from myself and to train others and spread the word.

My workouts for world records weren't the normal workouts. I could be lifting logs or sacks of coal in training and come home and not be able to move. If I ate too quickly after that, I was sick because my stomach wasn't settled. Samantha would cook the right food for me and rest my head on her lap to relax me.

The problem was that all this domestic bliss could soften me up when I should have been getting into a fighting mode. Samantha stayed away a lot before my last world record, so I could work on building up a certain amount of aggressiveness.

You can meet the right partner in life at the wrong time, but I met Samantha at the right time. She'd seen me on television but, unlike her two brothers, she wasn't really aware of what I'd achieved. She says that's probably a good thing. It wasn't until she started training with me that she began to feel proud she was being trained by a world-record-beater. I say she's brought stability into my life. I'm able to relax at home, even behave like a big kid. Before, I'd bring the tension of my training or instructor sessions back from the gym and into the house. Now I come back and there's a calmer atmosphere. It seemed strange at first to come home and begin to wind down, but Samantha would get the best out of me, even though I was feeling tense before going for a record.

Looking back at all the records I went for, my final record, with its ten events, was one of the toughest. I was going out on a high note but, at the same time, it was going to be bloody tough. I was training with a shoulder injury and a leg injury, and I couldn't wait to get that last record out of the way. My life was changing. I'd met somebody. That factor hadn't figured in my life before. I was happier to be staying in nights and eating the right food. And that was such an important part of training: your social life goes out of the window. You have to make sacrifices. But it drove me mad sometimes. Then again, it was nice to stay in with the right person.

When Samantha left the pop world, she went into the communications industry. But working for a company didn't give her the independence she needed and she soon realised she could do everything she was doing for herself. She started her own business with £100 about eighteen months before we met. That's all she had. She collaborated with her former boss and she generated the sales. Her company sells complete communication systems and cheaper calls and she undercuts the big companies. Her catchment area is from Manchester down to Oxford and Swindon and across to Wales. Two years after she'd started the company, they were doing half a million pounds in turnover.

So we're both achievers in our own fields. Samantha's made it financially and I've made it as a world champion. A top footballer gets £100,000 a week, whereas I've struggled in the past with the financial side. I've been prudent enough to save and invest, but it's been hard. Now I've retired from record breaking, I'm promoting myself more at a business level. And I'm not stupid. I'm even going to university part-time. The essays are a pain and Samantha sometimes laughs at my writing, but I'm determined to get my teaching diploma.

My university tutors are very supportive and it's certainly the right time to do this, because I reckon I'll have other commitments in a few years. Academically, I've known what it's like to be demotivated and I know this can result in problems later on. I'm taking time out for extra tuition on the essay side of the work. I accept it. And, this time, I'm motivated to do the necessary studying. But I've been busy with my other activities up until now. Maybe the teachers who taught me originally will have read about my record breaking in the press.

I started to look at a university education because, in spite of the experience I had for certain jobs I applied for, I needed extra qualifications. I had my NVQ as an assessor and management qualifications, but some jobs in the leisure business had asked for more. I rang the University of Birmingham and selected a course and got my interview. The first two modules I passed were research skills and project management; I thoroughly enjoyed the management module. The course had a good mix of individuals: some were studying for a degree and some were already involved in management and were there to improve their skills. There were a handful of postgraduates as well, from different backgrounds, mostly in management roles, and we were able to bounce ideas around. We discussed how to plan and prepare and delegate, how to deal with pressure and awkward situations. I'm always interested in leading roles. About nine years ago I did a course in Supervisory Management at Birmingham City College, which involved dealing with staff in a leisure complex at assistant-manager level.

I've just finished my psychology module and I chose an assignment on 'Hardship: the Preparation and Mental and Physical Aspects of an Athlete'. I used myself as a guinea pig. I couldn't have had a better source for research. I now have to pack in two modules a year for four years with the right number of credits for my diploma. There are a lot of new courses on leadership and challenge and I'm looking forward to doing those.

Local schools tend to look on me as a role model because of my world records. I don't think of myself like that. I see myself as Paddy. But, because of what I've done, people say I'm some kind of local celebrity. I don't feel I am. I don't think in those terms, though it goes with the territory. Boys and their fathers have queued up at events to get my autograph. I could see the light shining in the youngsters' eyes as I signed their copies of *The Guinness Book of World Records*. And Birmingham market traders sponsored me with fruit and veg for my training. That's working class for you: they supported me in that way. And I promoted the kind of health that comes from eating their type of food.

The local school has asked me to set up a course for pupils who are in danger of being expelled. They've invited me to come along as a motivator and instructor to do self-defence and community projects. It's similar to the Prince's Trust or Millennium Volunteers, and I was recommended to them. Other organisations can go into schools but, because of the way I deliver my knowledge, the school has asked for me personally.

And there are amateur athletes who say they've admired what I've done. They've wanted to train with me and get some hints and tips. I'm pleased to have their respect but I didn't take on world records for the glory. And I didn't do it for the press coverage or because of vanity. That's not my style. I did it because I wanted to break records. The rest was icing on the cake.

CHAPTER 14

TOUGH AT THE TOP

MY FAMILY ARE PROUD of what I've achieved. My brother, Declan, and my sister, Bridget, and my mother are the ones who are left in my family now and they've been pleased to leave me to get on and do the business. They come to all the events they can, but my mother is wheelchair-bound and it's not easy for her. She was determined to be there for my last world-record attempt on 25 November 2001. She's touching eighty, but she was an active and strong woman in her prime and totally appreciated what I was doing. I can see a lot of myself in my mother: she's a very stubborn person. She lives on her own but my brother and I look after her in different ways and go round to make sure she's all right. My brother lives round the corner and pops in to see her every day. I do the shopping and vacuum cleaning and she has a home help every morning to make sure she's OK and see that she's got a cup of tea. She has a nurse checking on her as well, because, although she can move, it's only slowly now. The main thing is, you've got to look after your mother.

Mum's seen me on television a few times but she's got bad eyesight now, cataracts. She prefers to listen to the radio and get feedback from the rest of the family. She talks to other people about me and she's proud of it all and pleased for me. I remind her of her own father, the fighter in the army. Her sister, my Aunty Carmel, looked at me the other day and said to her, 'Doesn't he remind you of our dad?' I do look a bit like him.

Declan was involved in sports like football and volleyball when he was in the army. But he married young and had children and that put paid to the sport. He's recently married again and he does a lot of walking and has a fairly active job. His wife, Annette, is an environmental health officer at Birmingham City Council.

Bridget has kids and lives back in Ireland now. It's a better life style for her. Ireland has a good quality of life and a high standard of education. The schools are very disciplined.

I wouldn't mind retiring to Cork myself. I made a lot of friends there when I did the world records in Ballycotton. The press covered what I did there and the well-respected *Cork Examiner* wrote articles on me more than once. I've been back a few times, seeing people and giving courses in self-defence, combat and fitness training in another fishing village, Cobh. It's a lovely, unspoilt part of the world.

* * *

When I was a child I didn't have any pets. I was probably too wild to have that kind of responsibility. Now I've got a dog, Carla, a Rottweiler. She's the first pet I've had of my own. Carla's twelve years old now. I got her eleven years ago from a Birmingham breeder. I was living alone and wanted a pet. Rottweilers are nice dogs to have around; they become very loyal. She's a cracking dog. She was the runt of the litter and kept getting bullied, so I picked her out. I love Rottweilers and when Carla passes on, I'll get another Rotter straight away. I didn't have to train her. I think dogs tend to know if you're in a good mood or a bad mood. Animals make good friends. They want to please. She's good with people but Rottweilers basically respond to one person. I wouldn't trust them in general. I only trust my own dog. Carla's great in the house and I'd trust her with Samantha but, if there were other people around, I'd be watching my dog.

If anyone raises their voice, Carla's ears go up, then back. She senses different vibes. She's also gone for a couple of people when she thought I was being threatened. Five or six years ago I gave a bloke a lift somewhere. He jumped into my car and Carla was sitting in the back. She nearly took his ear off. Missed it by an inch. Another time I was teaching at a leisure centre and a guy came up to me in the car park. 'Is that your dog?' he asked, clapping me on the back. Carla lunged for a moment. I didn't think anything more of it. As I drove off, I looked in the mirror and saw the guy jumping up and down, still holding his hand. I didn't realise the dog had bitten him. He had to go to hospital and have an injection, just in case. In the house, Carla's good as gold and wants to be made a fuss of. But, like any anyone else, if she's surprised, she reacts.

I gave myself my first tattoo at the age of eleven, with Indian ink. I was in a gang and we had to do our own tattoos. We didn't know what we were doing but it hurt like hell, stabbing yourself with a needle. So the first thing I had to do, when I was old enough, was get that marking covered up.

I've got tattoos on my arms, my legs and my back. I get them done locally in a shop called Hell's Angels. One of my tattoos says, 'Fit to Fight', because I believe that's what you should be. Another says, 'Out of Pain comes Glory', which I think is right. I've got two military tattoos on my back. And there's a knife design which says, 'Determination, Courage and Endurance'. But my tattoos aren't there for fashionable reasons. They relate to a genuine experience I've had; something I've achieved and wanted to put on record. It's a statement I'm making. Not a fashion statement, but a personal statement.

People are unsure how to take me when they first meet me. They're a bit wary of me, uncomfortable. Perhaps I come across as an aggressive person. Some people react by wanting to challenge me, because of my world records. That happens regularly, and often they're drunken individuals who are out to prove themselves in pubs and clubs. A person will come up to me and say something, and I'll simply respond by bawling them out. It shocks them and it's often enough to stop them in their tracks. You can get arrogant people in clubs who'll push you and take your drink when you're not looking. I still get verbal comments when I go out, and I think I'll have to put up with that for a few years to come.

In 1998, I remember, I was walking down the street one evening, on my way to a club in Solihull, when someone jumped on my back, then on the back of a friend of mine, for no reason at all. The guy was an amateur boxer from a local club and was, presumably, under the influence of alcohol. I went down on the ground and, as I turned round, I punched him in the eye and cut it. I also put some self-defence type of pressure on his eye socket which went straight through to the nerve endings in his head, so he let go of me. I got up and dragged him off the ground, even though he was bigger than me, and told him to get on his bike. It was an unprovoked attack from behind, but when I left him his eye was in a complete mess.

I've always believed in nipping situations in the bud. You don't let a confrontation continue because people will find a weak spot and take advantage. That goes for everyone in any walk of life. And not just in physical situations but in business negotiations as well. People will take advantage of a situation any time.

I'll always continue with my training. I may not maintain the level to which I've trained for my world records, but I'll keep fit. Only without a stopwatch. I can do half an hour in the gym now, and say, 'That's it,' and head for a sauna. But I'll go for more dan grades in the martial arts. At the moment I'm a fifth dan in unarmed combat and self-defence and a second dan with the

World United Martial Arts Association. It takes two or three years to get a dan grade; you have to go out there and get the knowledge and prove yourself. You don't just get a grading by going to a club. It's about learning and keeping fit; it's an ongoing assessment process. I should have completed my third dan with WUMA by autumn 2002.

The difference is, I won't have to carry logs or coal bags or run marathons with backpacks any more. I've proved myself. I can simply jog and bike and swim and focus on my boxing and martial-arts training. I'd like to combine the two fighting skills in the future.

When I have children, I'll teach them the martial arts myself, so they're enthusiastic about the sport. That's probably the only moment I'll seriously consider teaching kids, when I have children of my own. I reckon I'll understand them better. At the moment I'm happier to teach adults. But if I want my own children to take up the sport, I'll probably set up a kids' class to help them get involved. It would be the same whether I had a son or a daughter. I'd make sure my daughter had the confidence to walk down the street without being afraid.

I hope my children will be good all-rounders in sport, right from the beginning. It'll give them self-discipline, as well as self-assurance. I'd like them to go in for sports as individuals, where the pressure is on them personally. They'll appreciate the successes a lot more. It'll make them feel good about themselves. There's nothing wrong with putting a child under a bit of light pressure above a certain age, say fifteen years old. It's character-forming.

But, with sport and training, you've got to be careful of children's soft bones and allow them to develop and grow strong.

To me, competitiveness is a religion. I'm devoted to it. And that applies to things other than sport. To look at challenges and want to beat them. To be the best. The key is preparation: hard work in training. People don't see the blood, sweat and tears that goes on behind the scenes. You take a lot of pressure and get a lot of lumps and bumps in preparing for a world-record attempt. And there are setbacks all the time: injuries you have to worry about. In the months leading up to my final record attempt I was carrying an injury in my left shoulder. A muscle had snapped two months before the event and was only just beginning to heal. But I had to keep up my mental and physical strength in order to train for the record. I had to go out there and do it. Regardless.

Visualisation and goal setting are part of the preparation. It's self-motivation. You have to imagine yourself reaching the finishing line, or beating the clock or achieving a certain number of press-ups. You visualise this in the changing room. You know you can do it because you've already done it in your mind. You motivate yourself verbally and inwardly. I couldn't possibly go into an event if I had the tiniest doubt about achieving it. If there's an element of doubt, you shouldn't be there. It means your training's gone to crap.

And, if that's the case, look at your training methods, look at your coaches and get new people on board. I changed my training team over the years to give people a rest. These guys were there on a voluntary basis, helping me out, and they needed a rest so they could come back fresh. They put time aside for me and I appreciated that. I had to think like a project manager in that respect.

I didn't really talk about strength, speed and endurance events with other athletes who went in for world-record attempts. Everyone tended to keep hints and tips to themselves because they didn't want their record being taken off them. Some guys enquired about going for a record after I'd broken one. But some of the events I did weren't right for tall people. You need to be compact, five foot eight or nine, for some disciplines. If you're tall and you're trying to do squat thrusts, you've got more body to clear the lines. It creates a strain on the lower back, the hamstrings and the calves. A smaller guy can hunker down to the ground. Burpees are good for small guys to do. A six-foot-three person has to get his feet out and bring extra body weight in and push himself up again. I noticed that a lot of the people who competed in the same events as I did were more or less the same weight and height as me. I was the ideal shape for what I did. Endurance athletes today should be compact, solid muscle from the neck down.

I've been told I didn't produce any lactic acid when I was doing a world-record attempt. The body makes lactic acid when it's under physical stress, and that blocks the ability to continue. I do make lactic acid but I also have a high threshold of pain. A lot of athletes give up when they experience discomfort. It's mental attitude; it's about focusing. When I did my world records, the officials checked me out before and afterwards. I didn't have a blood test because I was in a minority sports category. But the only thing that was going round in my blood was the will to win, and that was down to preparation.

What I like to see when I'm watching other athletes is their level of staying power. I look at their age and can see that it's no barrier. Some people say, 'Oh well, I'm old now. I'm past thirty, so I can't compete.' That's a load of rubbish. Techniques and vitamins, as I've said, keep people competing into their forties and fifties in Masters and Veteran tournaments. Take the Masters Power Weight Lifting Championship; that's proof in itself that, in a lot of sports where stamina and endurance are involved, that age group has matured like a good red wine.

I'm very self-disciplined. To the highest degree. I run my life and my training in a positive way. Sometimes I can be lazy, like everyone else. But I've got so much going on in my life that I realise I can't give everything the same amount of input. At the moment I'm involved in running different courses for adult education: personal safety courses, fit-to-fight courses for doormen and bodyguard courses. I run martial-arts courses in my own gym and give one-to-one lessons on personal fitness to private clients. Besides that, I'm doing my physical education course, making fitness videos and compiling books, renovating my house and promoting my fitness work on the internet. I also hope to spend some time promoting martial-arts boxing equipment.

I get a lot of emails from military personnel in the States. Guys in Special Forces units, which are similar to the British SAS, often ask me about books and videos and training tips. They want help to improve their strength and speed and stamina to get them through their selection period.

When I was on holiday in Florida about ten years ago, I got on great with everyone there. I was talking to a guy about what I did and he said I should go on the local TV. The TV company came along and interviewed me and I was on one of their shows, demonstrating the kind of thing I did for world records.

But the best moments were in the winning. Then you could relax and say, 'Thank God, it's all over.' When I relaxed with the team afterwards, my trophy was a glass of champagne or a shandy. That was it. You could switch off. But then it was, 'Right, what's the next record attempt?' Back down the gym. Plan for it. Go for it. I never really had much time to sit back and enjoy and reflect on what I'd done. Even now, it's difficult to realise what I've achieved over the last fourteen years. Those one hundred and fourteen record titles.

I've got a quiet sense of achievement and satisfaction in what I've done, but I never set out to get this far. The plan wasn't there. The plan was one record attempt. Have a go. Then it escalated and became a professional athletic career, combining a variety of disciplines. I had no idea I had a range of sporting skills when I started out. I knew I was an all-rounder in amateur sports, but I never dreamt I'd reach world-class level. I found that out as I went along, by pushing the body a little bit further, then a little bit further. I didn't take drugs. The best drug for any event is the mind. It's more powerful than any steroid can be.

These last fourteen years of training and challenges have taught me a few things about myself. I can be a very abrupt sort of person. I find it difficult to tolerate people who put on an act. I'm not into falsity in social situations. I can get angry very easily, and I've learnt to channel that energy into training and taking the pain.

And there's no doubt about it: it was constant pain. But I learnt how to control that mentally. I've enjoyed the glory of winning, but it was only ever a short-lived celebration before getting back to training for the next event. Sport has given me self-discipline. It's kept me out of prison. If I hadn't gone down the sports road, I'd have gone down the prison road. And that would have been a one-way ticket for me.

I hope others will see how sport turned it round for me, how it helped me get my act together. They might say to themselves, 'Hold on, that guy's gone from there to here, from the dungeon and worked his way up to the first floor.' It could have gone the other way and, in fact, there was turbulence throughout the journey. I think I had too much energy to go in for mainstream sport. It wasn't challenging enough for me. I needed to go that extra mile.

Most of the records I achieved were established by someone else first. The challenge was to break those records. I always did my research, checking the books to find a record that would be of interest to a wide-ranging audience. My records weren't stunts; they were records at national, European and world level that were of widespread interest. From the moment you're shown how to do a press-up at eight years of age in a PT class, you're interested in how many press-ups someone else can do in a certain period of time.

Sometimes I was approached by associations, asking me to

establish a record in a new category. If you want to go for a new record, you have to go through the proper channels and get the approval of the record-book people or the appropriate association. You propose the record to an association, explain it hasn't been done before and ask if you can go for it. If it's a record that's achievable by others, if another person can challenge it, then the chances are you'll get approval.

One record I was asked to establish was the one-mile treadmill run on *Record Breakers*. The programme's production team had the idea for that. They'd seen my name in *The Guinness Book of World Records* and rang me up and asked me to come along.

When I was at school we did sport every day. We enjoyed a variety of sports and that's where I got my all-round skills. I started to develop a competence in sports when I went to my first secondary school, Jaffray. Mr Green was an excellent PT instructor; he knew how to teach and he put some time and effort into me. Soon I was doing trampolining classes after school and joining the school squad for championships. I only got a bronze medal in competitions but, at the time, I never thought I'd get that.

Mr Green also got me involved in athletics, so that I represented the school at senior school championships. Teachers are key people in a person's development. The best thing about this Mr Green was that he was actively involved in sport himself. He'd done it. He knew how far he could push a youngster to get the best out of him. Later on, when I was in my early twenties, I think I saw the guy once, and I'd love to see him again. He probably doesn't realise it, but he made a big contribution to the early stages of my sports development.

If I had to name the main influences on the coaching side of my career, it would be Mr Green, Ralph Farqharson, the Secretary of the British Amateur Weight Lifting Association and former champion and Guinness World Record holder, and Desi Clifton, a karate expert and football junior league team manager. Danny Ryan has also been a great supporter and friend, and he has excellent organisational skills.

I've had input from all of these people; anything from pushing me when I'm lagging behind to calming me down when I'm losing my temper. Richard Hopkins, the president of WUMA, has also been a big influence. His association has recognised me several times at martial-arts sports awards. He gave me the opportunity to go for the Warlords Black Belt Kumite World Title.

All these people are highly qualified and recognised as being at the top level in their own field. They're highly respected in their circles and I've picked up various pieces of knowledge from each of them and put it all together for my own needs. Added to this is the advice I've picked up from coaches on different courses and in different competitions over the years. Everyone is made up of a variety of influences and experiences, and these have been mine. The top people.

We've all noticed that children are getting fatter these days. One reason for this, I believe, is the comparatively small role played by sport in the school curriculum. And there was a time when children weren't encouraged to compete against each other. But life is one long competition. It's about survival. You're going to get knocked backwards in life. I've had my share of those blows from every direction: personally, financially and workwise. Some of it may have been down to me, losing my temper and getting worked up at the wrong moment, but I've got up off the floor and dusted myself down.

I feel that if more fitness and endurance sports are encouraged in schools, a lot of this new obesity will be checked. I still see a lot of my contemporaries, people I was at school with when sport was encouraged, and they're not overweight. But I see others who went to my secondary schools ten years later, who are only in their late twenties now, and they've got weight problems. They're drinking more and eating more fast food than we did. The takeaway mentality prevails.

It's what you're brought up with. Habits are formed at an early age. A hard childhood can make you tough, but you become a survivor. But children shouldn't be forced to compete if they don't have the right personality. You should never make them do something they can't or won't do. You try your best to encourage them, but that's all. Motivating a child is very important. Shouting isn't going to get you or the child anywhere. Parents who yell at their children that they should have done better are worse than anyone. I've seen it happen.

Goal setting, rehearsing an event over and over again in your mind, is an important part of going for a record. I always did this.

I imagined I'd succeeded in the challenge, that I'd crossed the winning line. Winning mentally is vital, and I learnt to do that over the years.

With my first record attempt, I was a bag of nerves. I was in the toilet, being sick. Even at my last record attempt, I felt sick. But feeling nervous and feeling the adrenalin are both natural reactions. If I wasn't feeling those things, I shouldn't have been there. It was part of the build-up to the competition. I was marching up and down in the changing room, and the team and officials were telling me to calm down. But, at the same time, I was rehearsing winning the record. I was focusing on the goal.

Training has developed a lot over the years; it's become more technical, more scientific, now. There are more sports therapists and you can get injuries sorted out straight away. There's an emphasis on stretching for flexibility. There's a greater awareness of nutrition and training programmes have improved. Twenty years ago athletes peaked in their twenties and early thirties. Now it can be the late thirties.

Cross training, having variety in your training programme, is important. It improves your stamina and gives all-round fitness and endurance. You can't beat cross training for explosive power. A lot of athletes still focus on their own sport and the training recommendations of their sport association. That's wrong. An athlete should be strong in different directions and at many levels. Doing different sports helps you to attain this.

* * *

I'm one of the few athletes who've turned fitness and endurance into a spectator sport. But luck hasn't been a feature in my life at all. It's been pure, bloody hard work behind the scenes. That's not luck, that's judgement. I've had injuries through training hard and they don't go away if you have to keep training. Sport is about sweat and hard work and going for it. It's about being tough, determined and dedicated.

There were a few moments, when my training was going wrong, where I got frustrated. As in any job, you get to a sticking point and you wonder for a split second if it's worth going on. So you say to yourself, 'I've had enough for today. I'm going to have a day off.' You get good days and bad days and moody days. And, if your training partners haven't turned up, there's nothing you can do about it. If you're not paying someone, you can't moan about it. Sometimes I had to go off and train on my own when I really needed someone to timekeep.

But my sports career moved forward on a pretty even keel. It was steady and so was the media coverage, both local and national. But that's because I worked for it. The first couple of years were the toughest. The challenge events were thought to be new. But what I was doing with endurance and speed records was already being seen on television with *Superstars*. This was a television programme where world-class athletes came together and competed against one another. These athletes were doing events in minutes, but I was doing something similar over a number of hours or days. The records were there to be broken and someone would come along every now and then and break one of them. But no one appeared to have turned record breaking into a career.

It's going to be another decade at least before a fitness and endurance athlete can earn a living from his sport. We have to wait for the competitions to be promoted before they become popular and lucrative. But there's more money finding its way into fitness and endurance sport now. Private companies and the National Lottery have helped. The leisure industry is a growing business. People are more flexible with their work hours, and often their firms have special arrangements with health clubs.

Now I've retired from competition, I prefer to go in the direction of giving courses and marketing. I don't think I have the personality for serving on a sports council. I'd probably have a disagreement with someone and I'm not one to mince words. I'm a hands-on and going-out-and-meeting-people type of person. I'm not an admin man.

My character has led me down a certain path in life. But I do believe you've got to be assertive, whatever you do. It's linked to the survival instinct. We've all got to flex our muscles to get on in this world. There are times when you've got to get a grip on things. We're all so relaxed and think we've done enough. That's where people have gone wrong. Every time I've thought that way, I've said to myself, 'No. I have to carry on.' You have to do as much as you can, or you're going to be a has-been. And in ten years' time you'll be saying to yourself, 'If only I'd made a bit more of an effort.' You'll always wonder if you should have done more.

I never say I hope I'll achieve something; I always say I will achieve it. I always think positively. I don't feel more at peace with the world than I did when I was younger. I'm still as I was; I'm still fiery. But there's a soft side to me; Samantha sees that, and my mother sees it, sometimes. I'm a private person and I keep my cards close to my chest. There's a lot in my life I'm never going talk about. No one will ever know.

CHAPTER 15

25 NOVEMBER 2001

I PUT MY SUCCESS down to being strong-minded, as well as keeping fit. It's about being hungry for success. Wanting to be the best. It's the same in the business world: if you want something and you put your mind to it, you'll get there. The most important thing is how you approach your goal. You can be hungry for something, but if you're arrogant about it, instead of being good to those around you, you're not going to get there. Wanting to achieve things in life is not about being an individual; it's a team effort. You have to be able to depend on people around you.

Even though I got into the boxing ring on my own and it was down to me to punch the hardest, I had a team to help me get there. They were with me, all around me. It was the same with my martial-arts challenges. I needed a team with whom I could spar and train.

* * *

For my final world-record attempt, on 25 November 2001, I trained in regular squad sessions with my team down at the gym for over three months. At each training session I did a couple of the ten events that made up the challenge, building up my strength. If there was a problem with the way I was doing press-ups or squat thrusts, we'd correct it there and then. It's too late on the day. My schedule meant I was training for five or six days a week. I always took one day off. You need to have a break. On a Sunday morning, along with the squad training sessions, we'd work on the log and coal-bag events. We'd always go for longer periods of time than I was aiming for in the challenge; going for, say, fifteen minutes with the log instead of five minutes. But I didn't race; I just took my time and built up my strength. If you start training early enough for an event, you can and should go a little bit beyond your goal in the challenge. That way, you're more comfortable when you go for it on the day.

Eight or nine hours' sleep, and I'm happy. My body and mind get a chance to repair themselves. For that last Fitness Endurance Speed Title, I'd be training for two hours in the morning and two hours in the evening. I started with the usual stretching exercises to improve flexibility, then a slow jog to warm myself up. After a workout you have to cool the body down with similar exercises, or you'll end up with cramp or muscle fatigue. And you have to keep the body warm when you finish by putting on extra clothes.

I trained mostly at my own gym or the Living Well health club at the National Exhibition Centre, depending on the equipment I needed to train on; I don't have a bike or a treadmill at my gym.

You have to listen to your body during training. If you go too far, you can ruin yourself for a record attempt. It was three or four weeks before the challenge that my calf muscle got badly torn during a four-mile run. The pain was extreme; it was as though someone had put a knife in my calf. I had it strapped up tight and had to rest it for a while. Fortunately it held out in training. But I was worried it was going to affect my performance on the day.

When you're pushing yourself in training, you're susceptible to all the viruses that are flying about. One of my greatest worries before any event was that I was going to catch a bug. I was always thinking: What if I get the flu? What if my back goes? I didn't need that.

Injuries are bad luck; they can happen to anyone. It's not a question of age. Athletes can injure themselves at eighteen, twenty-eight or thirty-eight. My back remained strong throughout all the weight-carrying events over the years. Any time there was a problem, I went straight to my sports therapist, Xen Yangou, and my osteopath, Ray Norwood. They helped me deal with the injuries I was carrying in the lead-up to my final record attempt. They didn't get rid of them, but they made sure I held up for the event.

It's possible I'll have a bit of arthritis later on, where I've been punched and kicked over the years and where I've had to lift and to run up mountains. I've been told that by my osteopath. I reckon it depends on how I look after myself from now on. I get a lot of comments about how I'm going to put on weight and balloon, now that I've given up competing. I don't think so. I'm going to keep training and continue to look at my diet. My body's used to being active and I've been told to keep up a certain level of training, especially for the first couple of years after I've retired. That's no problem. I enjoy exercise, even simple walking up hills.

Only once did a world-record attempt go wrong on me. That was in 1993 when I was carrying an injury. I was attempting a number of one-arm press-ups on Sky Television. I'd snapped my shoulder and I found I had no power there. But, even though I knew I wasn't going to break the record and get the number of press-ups required, I still continued for the full hour. I wouldn't give up. I had to finish. The way I looked at it, I wasn't a loser because I'd done the required hour of press-ups. But I was a thousand press-ups down. That's the difference an injury can make. I broke the record six months later.

The long road to my last record attempt began about seven or eight years before the challenge took place. I spoke to the head of the Human Achievements section at *The Guinness Book of World Records* and told him I'd like to go for a ten-event World Speed Fitness Endurance record. But we found other athletes had gone for similar records. Steve Sokel's record was reported in a national newspaper in 1994. It was a combination of strength, speed and stamina, and the guy was rated as the world's fittest man at the time. That was an immediate challenge to me. I'd been pitted against others in boxing and martial-arts events, but this would have been a dramatic challenge.

Desi Clifton wrote a letter to the newspaper to try to get Sokel and me together in a head-to-head challenge. But nothing came of it, and I couldn't wait around. I had to move on. We went ahead with other challenges, particularly the martial-arts kumite title where I had to fight a succession of different fighters. I had to be focused for that because I knew it was going to be a hard challenge.

There were quite a few challenges to Sokel's ten-event record around that time, one by a South African athlete. The concept was starting to develop as a challenge event. Sokel set another record about three years ago, something like ten events over twenty-two hours. He wasn't aiming for any particular time; he just completed everything in the fastest time possible. I think it included a thousand press-ups and a two-mile swim. He was enlarging the event and raising it to a new level.

I was busy doing other events, but in the back of my mind this 1994 record was there, waiting to be challenged. I suppose I was already thinking it would be my final event and I knew 2001 was going to be my final year. It seemed a good way to go out. The challenge took a lot of preparation, more than I thought it would. It was also the toughest record I'd attempted for a long time. It takes a lot of skill to train yourself up for ten different events. You have to be strong in different ways. I talked with my coaches, Desi and Danny, and we reckoned we could go out with a bang on this one.

I began training for 25 November after my previous event, in August 2001. I spoke to Stuart Claxton and Stewart Newport at

Guinness and we discussed what I wanted to do. There's a standard set of guidelines which you have to follow for record attempts. If it's an attempt in a new category, the officials decide on the guidelines and everyone follows them for each attempt after that. They look for the most repetitions in a given time for each event and the overall fastest time.

Even when a record has been achieved, the paperwork still has to be put together after the challenge and sent in. And not every record attempt that is accepted goes into the Guinness book. They have something like ten thousand records submitted to them every year, and sometimes you have to wait a few months for a reply, even if the record has been accepted. It goes on their database and they have thousands of certificates to send out.

All my records have been accepted by Guinness but the editors are not always able to put them in the book. Sometimes, when that happens, I'll submit the record to other books, such as the *Strength and Speed Record Book*. A lot of my boxing and martial-arts records have gone into the American book in that way, but you still have to go through the same process of submitting the right documentation. All the other books have rules and regulations which are as stringent as Guinness's, which is good.

During training there was no mincing of words with Desi and Danny. If there was a problem, there was a problem. If you weren't doing something well, you had to train again and get it right. If you hadn't prepared properly, you had to make sure you were prepared next time. They were blunt enough when they were helping me out, which was what I needed. It was the sort of language I was used to anyway. If anyone tried to beat about the bush, not talk in a direct way, they'd bore me. My coaches also knew when I should hold back. If I was going too fast with my press-ups or squat thrusts and I had got a lot more to do, they would slow me down and pace me.

But you can also get mentally drained thinking about different aspects of a challenge and wanting it to go well. You slip into a more dynamic gear, but it's a volatile situation: your moods vary. It's easy to get temperamental. You find yourself thinking less about people and focusing more on yourself. My body language changed and I could get quite aggressive. Sometimes my coaches would have to check me on that. But it's part of the build-up of adrenalin and part of the pressure. And all the time I was visualising my goal, my final goal.

Trust me to pick one of the hardest challenges for my last one. It really started to take its toll in my training preparation. I half-wished I hadn't decided on something so physically hard. But I wanted to go out the way I came in. Desi Clifton, Danny Ryan and Paul Jones would be there with me on the day, but it would be really tough. Ten different events, using every part of the body. Up until then I'd done challenges that had been demanding on different parts of the body at different times. But this last record attempt needed strength, speed and stamina combined on the same day.

Two or three weeks before the event, I went down to the Fox Hollies Leisure Centre at Acocks Green, where the challenge was to take place, to discuss the equipment with the officials. We made sure the seating for the audience was right and that the engineers could record the attempt properly. I chose the bike and rower from a range of equipment in the gyms run by Birmingham City Council and tried them out, so there would be no surprises on the day.

I was familiar with the hall; I'd taught courses and done a couple of record attempts there in 1990 and 1991. Matt Redmond OBE, the Labour Councillor who got the centre built for the local community, was going to be there to see my final challenge, and so was Ian McArdle, the Deputy Lord Mayor. Danny Ryan has also been awarded the OBE. He's involved in local leisure services and still runs and trains. He does a lot of marathons and hundred-mile bike rides to raise money for charity, especially to buy equipment for hospitals. All these people are genuine, down-to-earth guys.

I was slightly worried that my injuries wouldn't hold up on the day, and so were Desi and Danny. I'd torn a calf muscle and my shoulder was still playing up from my last record challenge, three months previously. In August 2001 I'd broken a tough world record at the Airborne and Special Forces Show at Bletchley Park, and I'd had to train for 25 November with the injuries from that. It was the first time I'd been badly injured before a challenge; I was normally injury-free before a record attempt. The muscle at the front of the shoulder had gone, and that's when you lose power. It wasn't as strong as it had been in the past, but I was determined not to screw up on my final challenge.

If it hadn't been for the injuries, there would have been no doubt in my mind that I would get the world record. I trusted my head but I wasn't sure how my injuries were going to behave. The challenge was all legwork and the first two events would tell if I was going to make it. The order of the events was planned so that I'd be as comfortable as possible during the attempt. You can do them in whatever order you want, and my sequence was different from Steve Sokel's record. I chose to get the most punishing events for my leg out of the way first: the shuttle runs, first with the bag of coal, then with the log.

My doctor told me I should have rested for two months; my osteopath said I should have rested for three months. And I was thinking, If my calf muscle goes in those early events, it's going to be a real struggle to go on. The way I looked at it, if I didn't get through the first two events, I would be under real pressure for the rest of the challenge. I had to do well in those two to put me on a roll, to give me confidence to tackle the others.

I didn't get up particularly early on the day of the challenge: about half-seven. I had some porridge and fruit for breakfast, drank some water and got my kit ready before the team came round to my house. You have to make sure your food is properly digested before a record attempt, or it can rise up and greet you when you don't want it to. I'd decided on the gear I was going to wear. It had to be comfortable: new trainers that grip, and absorbent socks to stop any friction. I greased my arms and my legs to stop any chafing. I'd learnt all about that the hard way.

We all set off together for the Fox Hollies Leisure Centre and got there around ten-thirty, with plenty of time to prepare. We installed ourselves in the changing rooms. You don't always get a changing room at a venue and occasionally I've had to change in a toilet. The City Council had set up all the equipment, ready for the event. After a meeting with the officials for the challenge, I did some stretching.

A lot of things were going through my mind in the changing room. I was a bundle of nerves, I was psyched up. But I was also getting nostalgic, knowing that I was coming to the end of a phase in my life. That is, until half an hour before the event. Then I became really focused. I was back into my usual tunnel vision, eyes on the goal. I played it through in my mind, how I'd achieve the record.

My sports therapist, Xen Yangou, helped me to loosen off my shoulders, my neck and my legs. He also strapped up my leg, ready for the event at one o'clock. I wasn't punching the walls, as I was before my first *Record Breakers* show. I'd got over that kind of nervousness. I was actually very focused. In the early days of world-record challenges, I used to go a bit wild. But you learn from experience. It's professionalism: channelling your energy into what you've got to do. My lowest pulse has been forty-five per minute, and the highest it's been when I've been competing is sixty-five. I fixed on preserving all my energy, both physical and mental, for those ten events. My breathing started to change as the adrenalin began to flow.

And we're off. Danny and Desi and my assistant coach, Paul Jones, are up there with me, along with the officials and the compère. The first event is the shuttle run, carrying a bag of coal weighing a hundred and sixteen pounds. I have to beat the previous best of seventeen times fifteen metres in five minutes. I begin. And the crowd are shouting for me already. I tell myself I won't let my snapped shoulder give way. I keep changing the bag from one side to the other, so the weight doesn't remain in one place. The clock is ticking; the crowd are shouting louder. Pretty soon the five minutes are up, and I stop. The MC speaks to the adjudicators. Then he announces I've carried the bag of coal for thirty times fifteen metres in five minutes. I've nearly halved the previous time.

But I'm straight into the next event: the shuttle run with the fifty-six-pound log. I have to beat nineteen times fifteen metres in five minutes. But my leg is playing up. My torn calf muscle, I can feel it going. Now my mind takes over; it cuts the pain. I've blocked it out; I've switched off. But, as always, I can hear my coaches. They're directing me, pacing me, encouraging me. The rest of the people out there, I can't hear at all. I block them out until the end, when their cheering will really lift me. Right now, I'm just looking down that tunnel to the light at the end.

The judges call time. I've carried the log for over thirty shuttle sprints in five minutes, beating the existing record of nineteen. But I'm not keeping count of what I'm doing myself. I'm concentrating on busting a gut, doing as much as I can and getting each event out of the way. Next comes the rowing event. The record is two hundred and sixty metres in five minutes. I row into the record books with nine hundred and ninety-six metres.

Now I'm on the bike. I've got to beat three-tenths of a mile in five minutes. But each of these events is tough in a different way. Someone wipes the floor with a towel under the bike. My sweat is forming puddles of water under the machine. Five minutes are up. I've made it: 1.39 kilometres.

On to the fifth event: the squat thrusts. One hundred and two to beat. I beat the record by doing one hundred and forty-four in five minutes. But now it's the treadmill run. I'm carrying a forty-pound pack on my back and I'm starting to struggle. My legs feel very heavy. I stop running and start walking. The crowd gasps. Then I pick up again. The record stands at two-tenths of a mile in five minutes. I come in at 0.39 of a mile.

The seventh event is the alternate squat thrusts. I nearly double the previous record of one hundred and twenty in five minutes with two hundred and twenty-five of them. But, next on the list is the burpees event. I'm getting tired. Those squat thrusts have really taken it out of me. I've got fifty-three burpees to beat in five minutes. I start. I hear my coaches. Then I pause for a moment. Both the alternate squat thrusts and the burpees are energy-sapping events. I'm really feeling it now. But the crowd roars me on. I'm there. Sixty-eight burpees.

I've reached the penultimate event. The record for shuttle sprints stands at three hundred and ninety metres. I nearly double that. I come in at six hundred and seventy metres in five minutes.

Now the tenth and final event. I need this for the world record. Non-stop punching and kicking the pads for five minutes. I have to be fast; I have to use explosive energy. At this point I'm starting to hear the crowd. I can appreciate the support. I let in all the noise in the hall and the people lift me. Paul Jones shouts the four shots I'm connecting with, and the adjudicator writes them down: 'One! Two! Three! Four!' The two punches and the two kicks are recorded each time. Everybody is shouting for me. The hall is in uproar.

There are four officials there, two from the Self-Defence Federation International, one from the Amateur Boxing Association and one from Birmingham City Council Leisure Services Department, all of them top-level instructors themselves, checking that I execute every move correctly. They have to make sure everything is above board and strictly adhered to because they sign the documents to be forwarded to the editorial team at Guinness. The challenge is also being videoed, in case the officials miss anything.

On this last event, when I hear everyone yelling for me, I feel great, over the moon. The crowd make a big difference. It gives me a real lift. It's good to hear the shouting, that support. It's a big psychological help. I break the record of seventy punches and fifty kicks on the pads with two hundred and three punches and two hundred and two kicks in five minutes. But what about my overall time?

I'd set out to beat the world record of one hour, twenty-one minutes for the ten events, and I did it in an overall time of fifty-eight minutes and forty-two seconds. I'd broken the hour. And I'd got through some of the events by quite big margins: I almost doubled the number of alternate squat thrusts of the previous record. It was the crowd support that lifted me. But the first feeling I had at the end of it all was simply exhaustion. I collapsed on the floor, getting my breath and slowing my mind down. I was overheating and I was mentally and physically drained. I'd given it my all. And there was a feeling of sadness that I'd reached the end of an era. I could see that one or two of my team had tears in their eyes.

It was the end of a bonding. We had memories. Ups and downs. We'd cracked jokes together, shouted and sworn together, been to the pub together. But all good things come to an end. I'd retired at the right moment. Constantly challenging world records puts a lot of pressure on the body and the brain. One hundred and fourteen of the world's toughest titles in different categories. I'm the only person to have done that. There are other athletes with about two hundred titles, but they're all for the same sport. It feels good to hold titles in different disciplines. I retired at the top of the ladder, as a world champion.

I felt elated. To receive that trophy and hold it in my hands was marvellous. But that was it, the end of an era. It was then I began to be conscious of my family and my friends who'd come to support me. But I was everywhere while people pumped my hand and clapped me on the back. You can't concentrate on anything after breaking a world record. The hall is a just sea of happy faces.

Someone wrapped a flag around my shoulders and I wiped my face with it, thinking it was a towel. I had to apologise for that. I always needed a towel and the team were constantly wiping the floor around me during an event. The MC shoved a microphone in front of me and asked me how I felt, asked me to comment. I can't remember what I said, except I thanked everyone and said I'd see them in the bar afterwards for a celebration. It was fourteen years of hard work, but I'd gone out as a winner.

My mum brushed away a tear. She was glad to be there but she was glad it was all over. She'd seen me go through a lot of pain over the years and she'd made a real effort to be there in her wheelchair for my last event. My sister remembered my first boxing bout, where she'd seen my nose get smashed in the second round. And my brother was there, smiling with his wife, just back from their honeymoon.

There was a great atmosphere back in the changing room. A lot of back-slapping and we opened a bottle of champagne. Later on, in the bar, I got up on the stage and presented plaques to all the people who'd helped me over the years. They deserved recognition as well. They'd stood by me at the gym and out in the rain and the snow. It was just a small token of my big thanks to them. A lot of people who get to the top tend to forget those who helped them get there. I'm not like that. I don't use people as stepping stones; I appreciate everything they've done. But they've had to wait fourteen years to hear it because I was busy with the record attempts.

In the bar, my body was still radiating heat and my metabolism must have been sky high. Even after a cool shower I was still sweating a couple of hours after the event. And my mind was still working overtime, making sure everyone was OK and thanking them for coming. After two or three hours we all went off to watch the event on TV. It was shown that evening on Central Television, which covers the whole of the Midlands. I got back home and cracked open another bottle of champagne with Samantha, then we went out for a quiet meal. But I was still on a high when we came back. I had to keep moving. I reckoned if I stayed still, I'd start reflecting too much on the end of my record-breaking career. But Samantha was her usual supportive self. 'You've got to move on, Paddy,' she said. And she was right.

I was down the gym a couple of days later, doing bag work and circuit training, even though I ached all over. I couldn't keep still, even though I felt burnt out. I'm the sort of person who needs goals. It's the constant training over the years that's kept me at the peak of fitness. I'm currently being assessed for my sixth dan with the Self-Defence Federation International, although the examinations won't be over until 2004. I'm also doing my third dan with the World United Martial Arts Association. WUMA are considered to have the world's toughest gradings. They really put you through it, physically and mentally. They push you to the limits, until you nearly break. When I get one of their grades, I really feel I've earned it. I still want to teach the martial arts, and to be an instructor. You've got to be on the ball yourself. I'll always be restless, looking for new challenges.

The twenty-fifth of November is over now. But, after a week of rest, I was still emotionally drained. It was partly the comedown, but I think fourteen years of going for world records had caught up with me. And there are fourteen years of memories, so I still feel slightly reflective. I think of the people I've met throughout my career. People like Roy Castle and Norris McWhirter. I'm happy to have achieved my final world record, but I'm sad it's all over.

Someone's just called. Wants me to go over to New York and spar at Gleason's Boxing Gym. Wants me to be a stand-in at their evening boxing show. The pain and the blood, sweat and tears aren't over yet. But that's another story ...